# Pictures from Brueghel

### and other poems

## By William Carlos Williams (in print)

The Autobiography (*Random House*)
The Build-up (*Random House*)
Collected Earlier Poems (*New Directions*)
Collected Later Poems (*New Directions*)
The Farmers' Daughters (*New Directions*)
I Wanted to Write a Poem (*Beacon Press*)
In the American Grain (*New Directions*)
Kora in Hell: Improvisations (*City Lights Books*)
Many Loves and Other Plays (*New Directions*)
Paterson, Books 1–4 (*New Directions*)
Paterson, Book 5 (*New Directions*)
Pictures from Brueghel and Other Poems (*New Directions*)
The Selected Essays (*Random House*)
The Selected Letters (*McDowell, Obolensky*)
Selected Poems (*New Directions*)
Yes, Mrs. Williams (*McDowell, Obolensky*)

# Pictures from Brueghel

and other poems by

# William Carlos Williams

*including*
**The Desert Music & Journey to Love**

**A New Directions Paperbook**

THE DESERT MUSIC AND OTHER POEMS
    Copyright, 1949, 1951, 1952, 1953, 1954, by William Carlos Williams.
    Reprinted by permission of Random House, Inc.

JOURNEY TO LOVE
    © Copyright, 1955, by William Carlos Williams.
    Copyright, 1954, by William Carlos Williams.
    Reprinted by permission of Random House, Inc.


Of the poems in this volume, the "Pictures from Brueghel" sequence
first appeared in *The Hudson Review*. Others appeared originally in the
following magazines, to which acknowledgment is here made:
*The Atlantic Monthly, Art News Annual, Botteghe Oscure, Chicago
Review, College Music Symposium* of the Moravian Music Foundation,
Inc., *East & West, Epoch, Folio, Harper's, Hudson Review, Imagi,
Kavita, The Kenyon Review, London Times Literary Supplement,
Massachusetts Review, National Review, New England Galaxy, New
Poems by American Poets, New Ventures, New World Writing, New
York Times Book Review, The New Yorker, Origin, Pennsylvania
Literary Review, Poetry, Poetry Australia, Quarterly Review of
Literature, Saturday Review, 7 Arts, Transatlantic Review.*

Acknowledgment is also made to The Lockwood Memorial Library,
University of Buffalo, and The Yale University Library for access
to their collections of Williams manuscripts.


Library of Congress Catalog Card Number: 62-10410.
First published as ND Paperbook 118 in 1962.
First Edition.
Manufactured in the United States of America.
Printed by The Golden Eagle Press.
New Directions Books are published by James Laughlin at
Norfolk, Connecticut. New York Office: 333 Sixth Avenue (14).

# Contents

# Pictures from Brueghel

". . . the form of a man's rattle may be in accordance with instructions received in the dream by which he obtained his power."

Frances Densmore
*The Study of Indian Music*

# Pictures from Brueghel

I   SELF-PORTRAIT

In a red winter hat blue
eyes smiling
just the head and shoulders

crowded on the canvas
arms folded one
big ear the right showing

the face slightly tilted
a heavy wool coat
with broad buttons

gathered at the neck reveals
a bulbous nose
but the eyes red-rimmed

from over-use he must have
driven them hard
but the delicate wrists

show him to have been a
man unused to
manual labor unshaved his

blond beard half trimmed
no time for any-
thing but his painting

According to Brueghel
when Icarus fell
it was spring

a farmer was ploughing
his field
the whole pageantry

of the year was
awake tingling
near

the edge of the sea
concerned
with itself

sweating in the sun
that melted
the wings' wax

unsignificantly
off the coast
there was

a splash quite unnoticed
this was
Icarus drowning

The over-all picture is winter
icy mountains
in the background the return

from the hunt it is toward evening
from the left
sturdy hunters lead in

their pack the inn-sign
hanging from a
broken hinge is a stag a crucifix

between his antlers the cold
inn yard is
deserted but for a huge bonfire

that flares wind-driven tended by
women who cluster
about it to the right beyond

the hill is a pattern of skaters
Brueghel the painter
concerned with it all has chosen

a winter-struck bush for his
foreground to
complete the picture  .    .

From the Nativity
which I have already celebrated
the Babe in its Mother's arms

the Wise Men in their stolen
splendor
and Joseph and the soldiery

attendant
with their incredulous faces
make a scene copied we'll say

from the Italian masters
but with a difference
the mastery

of the painting
and the mind the resourceful mind
that governed the whole

the alert mind dissatisfied with
what it is asked to
and cannot do

accepted the story and painted
it in the brilliant
colors of the chronicler

the downcast eyes of the Virgin
as a work of art
for profound worship

## V PEASANT WEDDING

Pour the wine bridegroom
where before you the
bride is enthroned her hair

loose at her temples a head
of ripe wheat is on
the wall beside her the

guests seated at long tables
the bagpipers are ready
there is a hound under

the table the bearded Mayor
is present women in their
starched headgear are

gabbing all but the bride
hands folded in her
lap is awkwardly silent simple

dishes are being served
clabber and what not
from a trestle made of an

unhinged barn door by two
helpers one in a red
coat a spoon in his hatband

## VI  HAYMAKING

The living quality of
the man's mind
stands out

and its covert assertions
for art, art, art!
painting

that the Renaissance
tried to absorb
but

it remained a wheat field
over which the
wind played

men with scythes tumbling
the wheat in
rows

the gleaners already busy
it was his own—
magpies

the patient horses no one
could take that
from him

Summer!
the painting is organized
about a young

reaper enjoying his
noonday rest
completely

relaxed
from his morning labors
sprawled

in fact sleeping
unbuttoned
on his back

the women
have brought him his lunch
perhaps

a spot of wine
they gather gossiping
under a tree

whose shade
carelessly
he does not share the

resting
center of
their workaday world

Disciplined by the artist
to go round
& round

in holiday gear
a riotously gay rabble of
peasants and their

ample-bottomed doxies
fills
the market square

featured by the women in
their starched
white headgear

they prance or go openly
toward the wood's
edges

round and around in
rough shoes and
farm breeches

mouths agape
Oya!
kicking up their heels

This horrible but superb painting
the parable of the blind
without a red

in the composition shows a group
of beggars leading
each other diagonally downward

across the canvas
from one side
to stumble finally into a bog

where the picture
and the composition ends back
of which no seeing man

is represented the unshaven
features of the des-
titute with their few

pitiful possessions a basin
to wash in a peasant
cottage is seen and a church spire

the faces are raised
as toward the light
there is no detail extraneous

to the composition one
follows the others stick in
hand triumphant to disaster

I

This is a schoolyard
crowded
with children

of all ages near a village
on a small stream
meandering by

where some boys
are swimming
bare-ass

or climbing a tree in leaf
everything
is motion

elder women are looking
after the small
fry

a play wedding a
christening
nearby one leans

hollering
into
an empty hogshead

Little girls
whirling their skirts about
until they stand out flat

tops pinwheels
to run in the wind with
or a toy in 3 tiers to spin

with a piece
of twine to make it go
blindman's-buff follow the

leader stilts
high and low tipcat jacks
bowls hanging by the knees

standing on your head
run the gauntlet
a dozen on their backs

feet together kicking
through which a boy must pass
roll the hoop or a

construction
made of bricks
some mason has abandoned

The desperate toys
of children
their

imagination equilibrium
and rocks
which are to be

found
everywhere
and games to drag

the other down
blindfold
to make use of

a swinging
weight
with which

at random
to bash in the
heads about

them
Brueghel saw it all
and with his grim

humor faithfully
recorded
it

## Exercise

Maybe it's his wife
the car is an official car
belonging

to a petty police officer
I think
but her get-up

was far from official
for that time
of day

## Song

beauty is a shell
from the sea
where she rules triumphant
till love has had its way with her

scallops and
lion's paws
sculptured to the
tune of retreating waves

undying accents
repeated till
the ear and the eye lie
down together in the same bed

## The Woodthrush

fortunate man it is not too late
the woodthrush
flies into my garden

before the snow
he looks at me silent without
moving

his dappled breast reflecting
tragic winter
thoughts my love my own


## The Polar Bear

his coat resembles the snow
deep snow
the male snow
which attacks and kills

silently as it falls muffling
the world
to sleep that
the interrupted quiet return

to lie down with us
its arms
about our necks
murderously a little while

## The Loving Dexterity

The flower
    fallen
she saw it

      where
it lay
    a pink petal

intact
    deftly
placed it

    on
its stem
    again


## The Chrysanthemum

how shall we tell
the bright petals
from the sun in the
sky concentrically

crowding the branch
save that it yields
in its modesty
to that splendor?

17

## 3 Stances

poised for the leap she
is not yet ready for
—save in her eyes

her bare toes
starting over the clipt
lawn where she may

not go emphasize summer
and the curl
of her blonde hair

the tentative smile
for the adult plans laid
to trap her

calves beginning to flex
wrists
set for the getaway


II: ERICA

the melody line is
everything
in this composition

when I first witnessed
your head
and held it

18

admiringly between
my fingers
I bowed

my approval
at the Scandinavian
name they'd

given you Erica after
your father's
forebears

the rest remains a
mystery
your snub nose spinning

on the bridge of it
points the way
inward


III: EMILY

your long legs
built
to carry high

the small head
your
grandfather

knows
if he knows
anything

**19**

gives
the dance as
your genius

the cleft in
your
chin's curl

permitting
may it
carry you far


## Suzy

I

women your age have decided
wars and the beat
of poems your grandfather

is a poet and loves you
pay attention
to your lessons an inkling

of what beauty means to
a girl your age
may dawn soon upon you

## II

life is a flower when it
opens you will
look trembling into it unsure

of what the traditional
mirror may reveal
between hope and despair while

a timorous old man
doubtfully half
turns away his foolish head

## III

a bunch of violets clutched
in your idle
hand gives him a place

beside you which he cherishes
his back turned
from you casually appearing

not to look he yearns after
you protectively
hopelessly wanting nothing

# *Paul*

### I

when you shall arrive
as deep
as you will need go

to catch the blackfish
the hook
has been featly baited

by the art you have
and
you do catch them

### II

with what thoroughness
you know
seize that glistening

body translated
to
that language you

will understand gut
clean
roast garnish and

serve to yourself who
better
eat and enjoy

however you
divide
and share

that blackfish heft
and shine
is your own


## Fragment

as for him who
finds fault
may silliness

and sorrow
overtake him
when you wrote

you did not
know
the power of

your words

## To a Woodpecker

December bird in the bare tree
your harsh cry sounds
reminding me

of death we celebrated by lamen-
tations crying out
in the old

days wails of anguish shrieking
wakes curses that the
gods

had been so niggardly sweet
nightingale of the
winter

woods hang out the snow as if
it were gay
curtains

## Song

I'd rather read an account
of a hidden
Carolina swamp where

the white heron breeds
protected from
the hunters reached only across

half-sunken logs a place
difficult of access the females
building their nests

in the stifling heat the males
in their mating splendor
than to witness

her broad pelvis
making her awkward at the
getaway . . .

but I have forgot beauty
that is no more than a sop
when our time

is spent and infirmities
bring us to
eat out of the same bowl!

## *The Children*

Once in a while
we'd find a patch
of yellow violets

not many
but blue big blue
ones in

the cemetery woods
we'd pick
bunches of them

there was a family
named Foltette
a big family

with lots of children's graves
so we'd take

bunches of violets
and place one
on each headstone

## The Painting

Starting from black or
finishing
with it

her defeat stands
a delicate
lock

of blonde hair dictated
by the
Sorbonne

this was her last
clear
act

a portrait of a
child
to which

she was indifferent
beautifully
drawn

then she married and
moved to
another country

## The Stone Crock

In my hand I hold
a postcard
addressed to me
    by a lady

Stoneware crock
salt-glazed
a dandelion embossed
    dark blue

She selected it
for me to
admire casually
    in passing

she was a Jewess
intimate of
a man I
    admired

We often met in
her studio
and talked
    of him

he loved the early
art of this
country
    blue stoneware

stamped on the
bulge of it
Albany reminding me
    of him

Now he is dead how
gentle he
was and
        persistent

## He Has Beaten about the Bush Long Enough

What a team
Flossie, Mary, a chemistry prof
and I

make to confront
the
slowly hardening

brain
of an academician
The most

that can be said
for it
is

that it has the crystal-
line pattern
of

new ice on
a country
pool

## *Iris*

a burst of iris so that
come down for
breakfast

we searched through the
rooms for
that

sweetest odor and at
first could not
find its

source then a blue as
of the sea
struck

startling us from among
those trumpeting
petals

## Song

you are forever April
to me
the eternally unready

forsythia a blonde
straight-
legged girl

whom I myself
ignorant
as I was taught

to read the poems
my arms
about your neck

we clung together
peril-
ously

more than a young
girl
should know

a burst of frost
nipped
yellow flowers

in the spring
of
the year

## The Dance

When the snow falls the flakes
spin upon the long axis
that concerns them most intimately
two and two to make a dance

the mind dances with itself,
taking you by the hand,
your lover follows
there are always two,

yourself and the other,
the point of your shoe setting the pace,
if you break away and run
the dance is over

Breathlessly you will take
another partner
better or worse who will keep
at your side, at your stops

whirls and glides until he too
leaves off
on his way down as if
there were another direction

gayer, more carefree
spinning face to face but always down
with each other secure
only in each other's arms

But only the dance is sure!
make it your own.
Who can tell
what is to come of it?

in the woods of your
own nature whatever
twig interposes, and bare twigs
have an actuality of their own

this flurry of the storm
that holds us,
plays with us and discards us
dancing, dancing as may be credible.

## Jersey Lyric

view of winter trees
before
one tree

in the foreground
where
by fresh-fallen

snow
lie 6 woodchunks ready
for the fire

# To the Ghost of Marjorie Kinnan Rawlings

To celebrate your brief life
as you lived it grimly
under attack as it happens
to any common soldier
black or white
surrounded by the heavy scent
of orange blossoms solitary
in your low-lying farm among the young trees

Wise and gentle-voiced
old colored women
attended you among the reeds
and polonia
with its blobs of purple
flowers your pup smelling of
skunk beside your grove-men
lovesick maids and
one friend of the same sex
who knew how to handle a boat in a swamp

Your quick trips to your
New York publisher
beating your brains out
over the composition
under the trees to the tune
of a bull got loose
gathering the fruit and
preparing new fields to be put under the plough

You lived nerves drawn
tense beside dogtooth violets
bougainvillaea swaying
rushes and yellow jasmine

that smells so sweet
young and desperate
as you were taking chances
sometimes that you should be
thrown from the saddle
and get your neck broke
as it must have happened and it did in the end

## To Be Recited to Flossie on Her Birthday

Let him who may
among the continuing lines
seek out

that tortured constancy
affirms
where I persist

let me say
across cross purposes
that the flower bloomed

struggling to assert itself
simply under
the conflicting lights

you will believe me
a rose
to the end of time

## Metric Figure

gotta hold your nose
with the appropriate gesture
smiling

back of
the garbage truck
as the complex

city passes
to the confession
or psychiatric couch or booth

## The Intelligent Sheepman and the New Cars

I'd like to
pull
the back out

and use
one of them
to take

my "girls"
to
the fairs in

## The Italian Garden

When she married years ago
her romantic ideas dominated
the builders

nightingale and hermit thrush
then the garden
fell into disuse.

Now her son has taken up her
old ideas formally
shut out

by high walls from the sheep run.
It is a scene from Comus
transported

to upper New York State. I remember
it already ruined
in

early May the trees crowded
with orioles chickadees
robins

brown-thrashers cardinals
in their scarlet
coats

vocal at dawn among pools
reft of their
lilies

and rarer plants flowers
given instead to
mallows

pampas-grass and cattails by
drought and winter
winds

where now hummingbirds touch
without touching.
Moss-covered

benches fallen apart among
sunken gardens
where

The Faerie Queene was read to
strains from
Campion

and the scent of wild strawberries
mingled with that
of eglantine

and verbena. Courtesy has revived
with visitors who
have

begun to stroll the paths
as in the quattrocentro
covertly.

Maybe it will drive them to
be more civil
love

more jocosely (a good word) as
we presume they did
in that famous

garden where Boccaccio and
his friends hid
themselves

from the plague and rude manners
in the woods
of that garden

as we would similarly today
to escape the plague
of

our cars which cannot
penetrate
hers.


## Poem

The rose fades
and is renewed again
by its seed, naturally
but where

save in the poem
shall it go
to suffer no diminution
of its splendor

## A Formal Design

This fleur-de-lis
at a fence rail
where a unicorn is

confined it is a tapestry
deftly woven
a milleflor

design the fleur-de-lis
with its yellow
petals edges

a fruiting tree formally
enough in
this climate

a pomegranate to which
a princely
collar round his

arching neck the beast
is lightly
tethered

## Bird

Bird with outstretched
wings poised
inviolate unreaching

yet reaching
your image this November
planes

to a stop
miraculously fixed in my
arresting eyes

## The Gossips

Blocking the sidewalk so
we had to go round
3 carefully coiffured
and perfumed old men
fresh from the barbers
a cartoon by Daumier
reflecting the times were
discussing with a foreign
accent one cupping his
ears not to miss a
syllable the news from
Russia on a view of
the reverse surface of
the moon          .          .

## Exercise No. 2

The metal smokestack
of my neighbor's chimney
greets me among the new leaves

it is a small house
adjacent to my bigger one
I have come in 3 years

to know much of her
an old lady as I am an old man
we greet each other

across the hedge
my wife gives her flowers
we have never visited each other

## The World Contracted to a Recognizable Image

at the small end of an illness
there was a picture
probably Japanese
which filled my eye

an idiotic picture
except it was all I recognized
the wall lived for me in that picture
I clung to it as to a fly

## The Fruit

Waking
I was eating pears!
she said

I sat beside her on the bed
thinking
of Picasso

a portrait of
a sensitive young boy
gathered

into himself
Waking
I was eating pears!

she said
when separate jointly
we embraced


## Short Poem

You slapped my face
oh but so gently
I smiled
at the caress

## Poem

on getting a card
long delayed
from a poet whom I love
but

with whom I differ
touching
the modern poetic
technique

I was much moved
to hear
from him if
as yet he does not

concede the point
nor is he
indeed conscious of it
no matter

his style
has other outstanding
virtues
which delight me

## To Flossie

who showed me
        a bunch of garden roses
she was keeping
        on ice

against an appointment
        with friends
for supper
        day after tomorrow

aren't they beautiful
        you can't
smell them
        because they're so cold

but aren't they
        in wax
paper for the
        moment beautiful

## Portrait of a Woman at Her Bath

it is a satisfaction
a joy
to have one of those
in the house

when she takes a bath
she unclothes
herself she is no
Venus

I laugh at her
an Inca
shivering at the well
the sun is

glad of a fellow to
marvel at
the birds and the flowers
look in

## Some Simple Measures in the American Idiom and the Variable Foot

I: EXERCISE IN TIMING

Oh
the sumac died
it's
the first time
I
noticed it


II: HISTOLOGY

There is
the
microscopic
anatomy

of
the whale
this is
reassuring


III: PERPETUUM MOBILE

To all the girls
of all ages
who walk up and down on

the streets of this town
silent or gabbing
putting

their feet down
one before the other
one two

one two they
pause sometimes before
a store window and

reform the line
from here
to China everywhere

back and
forth and back and forth
and back and forth


IV: THE BLUE JAY

It crouched
just before the take-off

caught
in the cinematograph—

in motion
of the mind wings

just set to spread a
flash a

blue curse
a memory of you

my friend
shrieked at me

—serving art
as usual


V: THE EXISTENTIALIST'S WIFE

I used to follow
the seasons
in this semi-northern

climate
and the warblers
that come

in May knew
the parula from
the myrtle

when I found it
dead on
the lawn there is

no season but
the one
for me now


VI: A SALAD FOR THE SOUL

My pleasant soul
we may not be destined to
survive our guts
let's celebrate

what we eject
sometimes

**49**

with greatest fervor
I hear it

also from the ladies' room
what ho!
the source
of all delicious salads




VII: CHLOE

The calves of
the young girls legs
when they are well made

knees
lithely built
in their summer clothes

show them
predisposed toward flight
or the dance

the magenta flower
of the
moth-mullen balanced

idly
tilting her weight
from one foot

to the other
shifting
to avoid looking at me

on my way to
mail a letter
smiling to a friend

VIII: THE COCKTAIL PARTY

A young woman
on whose belly I have never
slept though others

have
met today
at a cocktail party

not drunk
but by love
ignoring the others

we looked in
each other's eyes
eyes alert to

what we were saying
eyes blinded
breathless by that alone

IX: THE STOLEN PEONIES

What I got out of women
was difficult
to assess Flossie

not you
you lived with me
many years you remember

that year
we had the magnificent
stand of peonies

how happy we were
with them
but one night

they were stolen
we shared the
loss together thinking

of nothing else for
a whole day
nothing could have

brought us closer
we had been
married ten years

## The High Bridge above the
## Tagus River at Toledo


A young man, alone, on the high bridge over the Tagus which
    was too narrow to allow the sheep driven by the lean,
    enormous dogs whose hind legs worked slowly on cogs
to pass easily  .  .  .
        (he didn't speak the language)

Pressed against the parapet either side by the crowding sheep,
    the relentless pressure of the dogs communicated
    itself to him also
above the waters in the gorge below.

They were hounds to him rather than sheep dogs because of
    their size and savage appearance, dog tired from the day's
    work.
The stiff jerking movement of the hind legs, the hanging
    heads at the shepherd's heels, slowly followed the excited
    and crowding sheep.

The whole flock, the shepherd and the dogs, were covered
    with dust as if they had been all day long on the road. The
    pace of the sheep, slow in the mass,
governed the man and the dogs. They were approaching the
    city at nightfall, the long journey completed.

In old age they walk in the old man's dreams and still walk
    in his dreams, peacefully continuing in his verse
    forever.

## 15 Years Later

on seeing my own play
*Many Loves*
on the stage for the first time

I recall
many a passage
of the original con-

versations with my
patients, especially the
women, myself

the interlocutor
laying myself bare for them
all there

in the play but who will
take the trouble
to evaluate

the serious aspects of
the case? One
of the actors by

dint of learning the lines
by heart
has come to me

his face aglow openmouthed
a light in his eyes
Nothing more

## The Title

-as in Gauguin's *The Loss of Virginity*-
how inessential it is to the composition:

the nude body, unattended save by a watchful
hound, forepaw against the naked breast,

there she lies on her back in an open field,
limbs quietly assembled—yet how by its

very unrelatedness it enhances the impact
and emotional dignity of the whole . . .

## Mounted as an Amazon

She rides her hips as
it were a horse
such women

tickle me a pat answer
to philosophy
or high heels would

put them on their
cans if fol-
lowed up most women

are more pliant
come of
a far different race

**55**

## The Snow Begins

A rain of bombs, well placed,
is no less lovely
but this comes gently over all

all crevices are covered
the stalks of
fallen flowers vanish before

this benefice all the garden's
wounds are healed
white, white, white as death

fallen which dignifies it as
no violence ever can
gently and silently in the night.


## Calypsos

I

Well God is
love
so love me

God
is love so
love me God

is
love so love
me well


II

Love the sun
comes
up in

the morning
and
in

the evening
zippy zappy
it goes


III

We watched
a red rooster
with

two hens
back
of the museum

at
St. Croix
flap his

wings
zippy zappy
and crow

## An Exercise

Sick as I am
confused in the head
I mean I have

endured this April
so far
visiting friends

returning home
late at night
I saw

a huge Negro
a dirty collar
about his

enormous neck
appeared to be
choking

him
I did not know
whether or not

he saw me though
he was sitting
directly

before me how
shall we
escape this modern

age
and learn
to breathe again

## Three Nahuatl Poems

One by one I proclaim your songs:
    I bind them on, gold crabs, as if they were anklets:
    like emeralds I gather them.
Clothe yourself in them: they are your riches.
    Bathe in feathers of the quetzal,
your treasury of birds' plumes, black and yellow,
the red feathers of the macaw
beat your drums about the world:
deck yourself out in them: they are your riches.


Where am I to go, whither?
    The road's there, the road to Two-Gods.
    Well, who checks men here,
here where all lack a body,
at the bottom of the sky?
Or, maybe, it is only on Earth
that we lose the body?
    Cleaned out, rid of it completely,
His House: there remains none on this earth!
Who is it that said:
Where find them? our friends no longer exist!


Will he return will Prince Cuautli ever return?
Will Ayocuan, the one who drove an arrow into the sky?
Shall these two yet gladden you?
    Events don't recur: we vanish once only.
Hence the cause of my weeping:
Prince Ayocuan, warrior chief
governed us harshly.
His pride waxed more, he grew haughty
here among men.
    But his time is finished ...

he can no longer come to bow down before Father and
    Mother. . . .
This is the reason for my weeping:
He has fled to the place where all lack a body.


## Sonnet in Search of an Author

Nude bodies like peeled logs
sometimes give off a sweetest
odor, man and woman

under the trees in full excess
matching the cushion of

aromatic pine-drift fallen
threaded with trailing woodbine
a sonnet might be made of it

Might be made of it! odor of excess
odor of pine needles, odor of
peeled logs, odor of no odor
other than trailing woodbine that

has no odor, odor of a nude woman
sometimes, odor of a man.

## The Gift

As the wise men of old brought gifts
        guided by a star
                to the humble birthplace

of the god of love,
        the devils
                as an old print shows
retreated in confusion.

        What could a baby know
                of gold ornaments
or frankincense and myrrh,
        of priestly robes
                and devout genuflections?

But the imagination
        knows all stories
                before they are told
and knows the truth of this one
        past all defection

The rich gifts
        so unsuitable for a child
                though devoutly proferred,
stood for all that love can bring.

        The men were old
                how could they know
of a mother's needs
        or a child's
                appetite?

But as they kneeled
        the child was fed.

                    They saw it
and
        gave  praise!

            A miracle
had taken place,
        hard gold to love,
a mother's milk!
        before
                their wondering eyes.

The ass brayed
        the cattle lowed.
                It was their nature.

All men by their nature give praise.
        It is all
                they can do.

The very devils
        by their flight give praise.
                What is death,
beside this?

        Nothing. The wise men
                came  with  gifts
and bowed down
        to worship
        this perfection.

## The Turtle

*(For My Grandson)*

Not because of his eyes,
              the eyes of a bird,
                           but because he is beaked,
birdlike, to do an injury,
              has the turtle attracted you.
                           He is your only pet.
When we are together
              you talk of nothing else
                           ascribing all sorts
of murderous motives
              to his least action.
                           You ask me
to write a poem,
              should I have poems to write,
                           about a turtle.

The turtle lives in the mud
              but is not mud-like,
                           you can tell it by his eyes
which are clear.
              When he shall escape
                           his present confinement
he will stride about the world
              destroying all
                           with his sharp beak.
Whatever opposes him
              in the streets of the city
                           shall go down.
Cars will be overturned.
              And upon his back
                           shall ride,

to his conquests,
      my Lord,
            you!

You shall be master!
      In the beginning
            there was a great tortoise
who supported the world.
      Upon him
            all ultimately
rests.
      Without him
            nothing will stand.
He is all wise
      and can outrun the hare.
            In the night
his eyes carry him
      to unknown places.
            He is your friend.

## Sappho, Be Comforted

There is only one love
let it be a sparrow
to hold between the breasts
        greets us daily with its small cries

what does it matter?
I, we'll say, love a woman
but truth to tell
        I love myself more. Sappho loves

the music of her own
songs which men seldom
mean to her, a lovely girl
        of whom she is desperately fond:

This is myself though
my hateful mirror
shows every day my big nose.
        Men are indifferent to me, my sweet

but I would not trade
my skill in composition for
all, a second choice, you
        present for my passionate caresses.

## To My Friend Ezra Pound

or he were a Jew or a
Welshman
I hope they do give you the Nobel Prize
it would serve you right
            —in perpetuity
with such a name

If I were a dog
I'd sit down on a cold pavement
in the rain
to wait for a friend (and so would you)
if it so pleased me
even if it were January or Zukofsky

Your English
is not specific enough
As a writer of poems
you show yourself to be inept not to say
usurious

## Tapiola

He is no more dead than Finland herself is dead
under the blows of the mass-man who threatened
to destroy her until she felled her forests
about his head, ensnaring him. But, children, you
underestimated the power in your own song, *Finlandia!*
It holds you up but no more so than has he I celebrate
who had heard the icy wind in his ears and defied
it lovingly with a smile. The power of music,
of composition, the placing of sounds together,
edge against edge, Musorgski the half-mad Russian
had it and Dostoevski who knew the soul. In such
style whistled the winds grateful to be tamed,
we say, by a man. Whee-wow! You stayed up half
the night in your attic room under the eaves, composing
secretly, setting it down, period after period,
as the wind whistled. Lightning flashed! The roof
creaked about your ears threatening to give
way! But you had a composition to finish that could
not wait. The storm entered your mind where all
good things are secured, written down, for love's
sake and to defy the devil of emptiness. The
children are decked out in ribbons, bunting and
with flags in their hands to celebrate your birthday!
They parade to music! a joyous occasion. Sibelius
has been born and continues to live in all our
minds, all of us, forever. . . .

## Poem

The plastic surgeon who has
concerned himself
with the repair of the mole

on my ear could not be
more pointedly
employed

let all men confess it
Gauguin or Van Gogh
were intimates

who fell out finally
and parted going
to the ends of the earth

to be apart, wild men
one of them cut
his ear off with a pair of shears

which made him none the less
a surpassing genius
this happened

yesterday forgive him
he was mad
and who among us has retained

his sanity or balance
in the course the
events have taken since those days

## Heel & Toe to the End

Gagarin says, in ecstasy,
he could have
gone on forever

he floated
ate and sang
and when he emerged from that

one hundred eight minutes off
the surface of
the earth he was smiling

Then he returned
to take his place
among the rest of us

from all that division and
subtraction a measure
toe and heel

heel and toe he felt
as if he had
been dancing

## The Rewaking

Sooner or later
we must come to the end
of striving

to re-establish
the image the image of
the rose

but not yet
you say extending the
time indefinitely

by
your love until a whole
spring

rekindle
the violet to the very
lady's-slipper

and so by
your love the very sun
itself is revived

# The Desert Music and Other Poems

*(1954)*

*To Bill and Paul*

## The Descent

The descent beckons
             as the ascent beckoned.
                       Memory is a kind
of accomplishment,
            a sort of renewal
                even
an initiation, since the spaces it opens are new places
            inhabited by hordes
                    heretofore unrealized,
of new kinds—
            since their movements
                  are toward new objectives
(even though formerly they were abandoned).


No defeat is made up entirely of defeat—since
the world it opens is always a place
            formerly
                  unsuspected. A
world lost,
            a world unsuspected,
                beckons to new places
and no whiteness (lost) is so white as the memory
of whiteness    .


With evening, love wakens
            though its shadows
                which are alive by reason
of the sun shining—
            grow sleepy now and drop away
                from desire    .

Love without shadows stirs now
                beginning to awaken
                                as night
advances.


The descent
                made up of despairs
                                and without accomplishment
realizes a new awakening:
                                which is a reversal
of despair.
                For what we cannot accomplish, what
is denied to love,
                what we have lost in the anticipation—
                                a descent follows,
endless and indestructible .

## To Daphne and Virginia

The smell of the heat is boxwood
        when rousing us
                a movement of the air
stirs our thoughts
        that had no life in them
                to a life, a life in which
two women agonize:
        to live and to breathe is no less.
                Two young women.
The box odor
        is the odor of that of which
                partaking separately,
each to herself
        I partake also
       .    .      separately.


Be patient that I address you in a poem,
        there is no other
                fit medium.
The mind
        lives there. It is uncertain,
                can trick us and leave us
agonized. But for resources
        what can equal it?
                There is nothing. We
should be lost
        without its wings to
                fly off upon.


The mind is the cause of our distresses
        but of it we can build anew.
                Oh something more than

it flies off to:
                a woman's world,
                        of crossed sticks, stopping
thought. A new world
                is only a new mind.
                        And the mind and the poem
are all apiece.
                Two young women
                        to be snared,
odor of box,
                to bind and hold them
                        for the mind's labors.


All women are fated similarly
                facing men
                        and there is always
another, such as I,
                who loves them,
                        loves all women, but
finds himself, touching them,
                like other men,
                        often confused.


I have two sons,
                the husbands of these women,
                        who live also
in a world of love,
                apart.
                        Shall this odor of box in
                        the heat
not also touch them
                fronting a world of women
                        from which they are
debarred
                by the very scents which draw them on
                        against easy access?

In our family we stammer unless,
              half mad,
                          we come to speech at last

And I am not
              a young man.
                          My love encumbers me.
It is a love
              less than
                          a young man's love but,
like this box odor
              more penetrant, infinitely
                          more penetrant,
in that sense not to be resisted.

There is, in the hard
              give and take
                          of a man's life with
                          a woman
a thing which is not the stress itself
              but beyond
                          and above
that,
              something that wants to rise
              and shake itself
free. We are not chickadees
              on a bare limb
                          with a worm in the mouth.
The worm is in our brains
              and concerns them
                          and not food for our
offspring, wants to disrupt
              our thought
                          and throw it
to the newspapers
              or anywhere.

There is, in short,
a counter stress,
                    born of the sexual shock,
                              which survives it
consonant with the moon,
                    to keep its own mind.
                              There is, of course,
more.
                    Women
                              are not alone
in that. At least
                    while this healing odor is abroad
                              one can write a poem.


Staying here in the country
                    on an old farm
                              we eat our breakfasts
on a balcony under an elm.
                    The shrubs below us
                              are neglected. And
there, penned in,
                    or he would eat the garden,
                              lives a pet goose who
tilts his head
                    sidewise
                              and looks up at us,
a very quiet old fellow
                    who writes no poems.
                              Fine mornings we sit there
while birds
                    come and go.
                              A pair of robins
is building a nest      .
                    for the second time
                              this season. Men

against their reason
        speak of love, sometimes,
                when they are old. It is
all they can do      .
        or watch a heavy goose
            who waddles, slopping
            noisily in the mud of
            his pool.

## The Orchestra

The precise counterpart
            of a cacophony of bird calls
                        lifting the sun almighty
into his sphere: wood-winds
            clarinet and violins
                        sound a prolonged A!
Ah! the sun, the sun! is about to rise
            and shed his beams
                        as he has always done
upon us all,
            drudges and those
                        who live at ease,
women and men,
            upon the old,
                        upon children and the sick
who are about to die and are indeed
            dead in their beds,
                        to whom his light
is forever lost. The cello
            raises his bass note
                        manfully in the treble din:
Ah, ah and ah!
            together, unattuned
                        seeking a common tone.
Love is that common tone
            shall raise his fiery head
                        and sound his note.

The purpose of an orchestra
            is to organize those sounds
                        and hold them
to an assembled order        .
            in spite of the

"wrong note." Well, shall we
think or listen? Is there a sound addressed
            not wholly to the ear?
                  We half close
our eyes. We do not
            hear it through our eyes.
                  It is not
a flute note either, it is the relation
            of a flute note
                  to a drum. I am wide
awake. The mind
            is listening. The ear
                  is alerted. But the ear
in a half-reluctant mood
            stretches
                  .     .     and yawns.


And so the banked violins
            in three tiers
                  enliven the scene,
pizzicato. For a short
            memory or to
                  make the listener listen
the theme is repeated
            stressing a variant:
                  it is a principle of music
to repeat the theme. Repeat
            and repeat again,
                  as the pace mounts. The
theme is difficult     .
            but no more difficult
                  than the facts to be
resolved. Repeat
            and repeat the theme
                  and all it develops to be

until thought is dissolved
in tears.
Our dreams
have been assaulted
by a memory that will not
sleep. The
French horns
interpose
.   .    their voices:
I love you. My heart
is innocent. And this
the first day of the world!

Say to them:
"Man has survived hitherto because he was too ignorant
to know how to realize his wishes. Now that he can realize
them, he must either change them or perish."

Now is the time   .
in spite of the "wrong note"
I love you. My heart is
innocent.
And this the first
(and last) day of the world

The birds twitter now anew
but a design
surmounts their twittering.
It is a design of a man
that makes them twitter.
It is a design.

## For Eleanor and Bill Monahan

Mother of God! Our Lady!
     the heart
          is an unruly Master:
Forgive us our sins
     as we
          forgive
those who have sinned against
     us.
          We submit ourselves
to Your rule
     as the flowers in May
          submit themselves to
          Your Holy rule—against
that impossible springtime
     when men
          shall be the flowers
spread at your feet.

As far as spring is
     from winter
          so are we
from you now. We have not come
     easily
          to your environs
but painfully
     across sands
          that have scored our
feet. That which we have suffered
     was for us
          to suffer. Now,
in the winter of the year,
     the birds who know how
          to escape suffering

by flight
                are gone. Man alone
                        is that creature who
cannot escape suffering
                by flight        .

I do not come to you
                save that I confess
                        to being
                        half man and half
woman. I have seen the ivy
                cling
                        to a piece of crumbled
wall so that
                you cannot tell
                        by which either
stands: this is to say
                if she to whom I cling
                        is loosened both
of us go down.

Mother of God
                I have seen you stoop
                        to a merest flower
and raise it
                and press it to your cheek.
                        I could have called out
joyfully
                but you were too far off.
                        You are a woman and
it was
                a woman's gesture.

You have no lovers now
                in the bare skies
                        to bring you flowers,

to whisper to you
        under a hedge
                howbeit
you are young
        and fit to be loved.
                I declare it boldly
with my heart
        in my teeth
                and my knees knocking
together. Yet I declare
        it, and by God's word
                it is no lie. Make us
humble and obedient to His rule.

There are men
        who as they live
                fling caution to the
wind and women praise them
        and love them for it.
                Cruel as the claws of
a cat        .        .

The moon which
        they have vulgarized recently
                is still
your planet
        as it was Dian's before
                you. What
do they think they will attain
        by their ships
                that death has not
already given
        them? Their ships
                should be directed
inward upon        .        But I
        am an old man. I
                have had enough.

The female principle of the world
      is my appeal
              in the extremity
to which I have come.
        *O clemens! O pia! O dolcis!*
        *Maria!*

## To a Dog Injured in the Street

It is myself,
      not the poor beast lying there
         yelping with pain
that brings me to myself with a start—
      as at the explosion
         of a bomb, a bomb that has laid
all the world waste.
      I can do nothing
         but sing about it
and so I am assuaged
      from my pain.

A drowsy numbness drowns my sense
      as if of hemlock
         I had drunk. I think
of the poetry
      of René Char
         and all he must have seen
and suffered
      that has brought him
         to speak only of

sedgy rivers,
                of daffodils and tulips
                        whose roots they water,
even to the free-flowing river
                that laves the rootlets
                        of those sweet-scented flowers
that people the
                milky
                        way       .


I remember Norma
                our English setter of my childhood
                        her silky ears
and expressive eyes.
                She had a litter
                        of pups one night
in our pantry and I kicked
                one of them
                        thinking, in my alarm,
that they
                were biting her breasts
                        to destroy her.


I remember also
                a dead rabbit
                        lying harmlessly
on the outspread palm
                of a hunter's hand.
                        As I stood by
watching
                he took a hunting knife
                        and with a laugh
thrust it
                up into the animal's private parts.
                        I almost fainted.

Why should I think of that now?
        The cries of a dying dog
                are to be blotted out
as best I can.
        René Char
                you are a poet who believes
in the power of beauty
        to right all wrongs.
                I believe it also.
With invention and courage
        we shall surpass
                the pitiful dumb beasts,
let all men believe it,
        as you have taught me also
                to believe it.

# The Yellow Flower

What shall I say, because talk I must?
    That I have found a cure
        for the sick?
I have found no cure
    for the sick    .
        but this crooked flower
which only to look upon
    all men
        are cured. This
is that flower
    for which all men
        sing secretly their hymns
of praise. This
    is that sacred
        flower!

Can this be so?
    A flower so crooked
        and obscure? It is
a mustard flower
    and not a mustard flower,
        a single spray
topping the deformed stem
    of fleshy leaves
        in this freezing weather
under glass.

An ungainly flower and
    an unnatural one,
        in this climate; what
can be the reason
    that it has picked me out
        to hold me, openmouthed,

rooted before this window
                in the cold,
                        my will
drained from me
            so that I have only eyes
                        for these yellow,
twisted petals    .    ?


That the sight,
            though strange to me,
                    must be a common one,
is clear: there are such flowers
            with such leaves
                    native to some climate
which they can call
            their own.


But why the torture
            and the escape through
                    the flower? It is
as if Michelangelo
            had conceived the subject
                    of his *Slaves* from this
—or might have done so.
                And did he not make
                    the marble bloom? I
am sad
        as he was sad
                in his heroic mood.
But also
            I have eyes
                    that are made to see and if
they see ruin for myself
            and all that I hold
                    dear, they see

also
               through the eyes
                       and through the lips
and tongue the power
        to free myself
               and speak of it, as
Michelangelo through his hands
        had the same, if greater,
               power.


Which leaves, to account for,
        the tortured bodies
               of
the slaves themselves
        and
               the tortured body of my flower
which is not a mustard flower at all
        but some unrecognized
               and unearthly flower
for me to naturalize
        and acclimate
               and choose it for my own.

## The Host

According to their need,
             this tall Negro evangelist
                           (at a table separate from the
                           rest of his party);
these two young Irish nuns
             (to be described subsequently);
                           and this white-haired Anglican
have come witlessly
             to partake of the host
                           laid for them (and for me)
by the tired waitresses.

It is all
             (since eat we must)
                           made sacred by our common need.
The evangelist's assistants
             are most open in their praise
                           though covert
as would be seemly
             in such a public
                           place. The nuns
are all black, a side view.
             The cleric,
                           his head bowed to reveal
his unruly poll
             dines alone.

My eyes are restless.
             The evangelists eat well,
                           fried oysters and what not
at this railway restaurant. The Sisters
             are soon satisfied. One
                           on leaving,

looking straight before her under steadfast brows,
        reveals
                blue eyes. I myself
have brown eyes
        and a milder mouth.

There is nothing to eat,
        seek it where you will,
                but of the body of the Lord.
The blessed plants
        and the sea, yield it
                to the imagination
intact. And by that force
        it becomes real,
                bitterly
to the poor animals
        who suffer and die
                that we may live.

The well-fed evangels,
        the narrow-lipped and bright-eyed nuns,
                the tall,
white-haired Anglican,
        proclaim it by their appetites
                as do I also,
chomping with my worn-out teeth:
        the Lord is my shepherd
                I shall not want.

No matter how well they are fed,
        how daintily
                they put the food to their lips,
it is all
        according to the imagination!
Only the imagination
        is real! They have imagined it,

                    therefore it is so:
of the evangels,
                with the long legs characteristic of the race—
                    only the docile women
of the party smiled at me
                when, with my eyes
                        I accosted them.
The nuns—but after all
                I saw only a face, a young face
                    cut off at the brows.
It was a simple story.
                The cleric, plainly
                        from a good school,
interested me more,
                a man with whom I might
                        carry on a conversation.


No one was there
                save only for
                        the food. Which I alone,
being a poet,
                could have given them.
                    But I
had only my eyes
                with which to speak.

## Deep Religious Faith

Past death
            past rainy days
                        or the distraction
of lady's-smocks all silver-white;
                        beyond the remote borders
                                    of poetry itself
if it does not drive us,
                        it is vain.
                                    Yet it is
that which made El Greco
                        paint his green and distorted saints
                                    and live
lean.
                        It is what in life drives us
                                    to praise music
and the old
                        or sit by a friend
                                    in his last hours.


All that which makes the pear ripen
                        or the poet's line
                                    come true!
Invention is the heart of it.

Without the quirks
                        and oddnesses of invention
                                    the paralytic is confirmed
in his paralysis,
                        it is from a northern
                                    and half-savage country
where the religion
            is hate.

                    There
the citizens are imprisoned.
            The rose
                    may not be worshipped
or the poet look to it
            for benefit.


In the night a
            storm of gale proportions came
            up.
                    No one was there to envisage
a field of daisies!
            There were bellowings
                    and roarings
from a child's book
            of fairy tales,
                    the rumble
of a distant bombing
            —or of a bee!
                    Shame on our poets,
they have caught the prevalent fever:
            impressed
                    by the "laboratory,"
they have forgot
            the flower!
                    which goes beyond all
laboratories!
            They have quit the job
                    of invention. The
imagination has fallen asleep
            in a poppy-cup.

# The Mental Hospital Garden

It is far to Assisi,
 but not too far:
  Over this garden,
brooding over this garden,
  there is a kindly spirit,
   brother to the poor
and who is poorer than he
  who is in love
   when birds are nesting
in the spring of the year?
  They came
   to eat from his hand
who had nothing,
  and yet
   from his plenty
he fed them all.
  All mankind
   grew to be his debtors,
a simple story.
  Love is in season.

At such a time,
  hyacinth time
   in
the hospital garden,
  the time
   of the coral-flowered
and early salmon-pink
  clusters, it is
   the time also of
abandoned birds' nests
  before
   the sparrows start
   to tear them apart

against the advent of that bounty
                from  which
                                they will build anew.


All about them
                on the lawns
                                the young couples
embrace        .
                as in a tale
                                by Boccaccio.
They are careless
                under license of the disease
                                which has restricted them
to these grounds.
                St. Francis forgive them
                                and all lovers
whoever they may be.
                They have seen
                                a great light, it
springs from their own bawdy foreheads.
                The light
                                is sequestered there
by these enclosing walls.
                They are divided
                                from their fellows.
It is a bounty
                from a last year's bird's nest.
                                St. Francis,
who befriended the wild birds,
                by their aid,
                                those who
have nothing
                and live
                                by the Holy light of love
that rules,
                blocking despair,
                                over this garden.

Time  passes.
                    The pace has slackened
                              But with the falling off
of the pace
              the scene has altered.
                              The lovers raise their heads,
at that which has come over them.
              It is summer now.
                              The broad sun
shines!
              Blinded by the light
                         they walk bewildered,
seeking
              between the leaves
                         for a vantage
from which to view
              the advancing season.
                              They are incredulous
of their own cure
              and half minded
                         to escape
into the dark again.
              The scene
                         indeed has changed.
By St. Francis
              the whole scene
                         has changed.
They glimpse
              a surrounding sky
                         and the whole countryside.
Filled with terror
              they seek
                         a familiar flower
at which to warm themselves,
              but the whole field
                         accosts them.
They hide their eyes

                    ashamed
                              before that bounty,
peering through their fingers
                    timidly.
                              The saint is watching,
his eyes filled with pity.


The year is still young
                    but not so young
                              as they
who face the fears
          with which
                    they are confronted.
Reawakened
          after love's first folly
                    they resemble children
roused from a long sleep.
          Summer is here,
                    right enough.
The saint
          has tactfully withdrawn.
                    One
emboldened,
          parting the leaves before her,
                    stands in the full sunlight,
alone
          shading her eyes
                    as her heart
beats wildly
          and her mind
                    drinks up
the full meaning
          of it
                    all!

## The Artist

Mr. T.
         bareheaded
                    in a soiled undershirt
his hair standing out
         on all sides
                    stood on his toes
heels together
         arms gracefully
                    for the moment
curled above his head.
         Then he whirled about
                    bounded
into the air
         and with an *entrechat*
                    perfectly achieved
completed the figure.
         My mother
                    taken by surprise
where she sat
         in her invalid's chair
                    was left speechless.
Bravo! she cried at last
         and clapped her hands.
                    The man's wife
came from the kitchen:
         What goes on here? she said.
                    But the show was over.

# Theocritus: Idyl I

*A Version from the Greek*

The whisper of the wind in
        that pine tree,
                goatherd,
is sweet as the murmur of live water;
        likewise
                your flute notes. After Pan
you shall bear away second prize.
        And if he
                take the goat
with the horns,
        the she-goat
                is yours: but if
he choose the she-goat,
        the kid will fall
                to your lot.
And the flesh of the kid
        is dainty
                before they begin milking them.

**GOATHERD**

Your song is sweeter,
        shepherd,
                than the music
of the water as it plashes
        from the high face
                of yonder rock!
If the Muses

choose the young ewe
                    you shall receive
a stall-fed lamb
            as your reward,
                    but if
they prefer the lamb
            you
                        shall have the ewe for
                        second prize.


**THYRSIS**

Will you not, goatherd,
            in the Nymph's name
                        take your place on this
                        sloping knoll
among the tamarisks
            and pipe for me
                        while I tend my sheep.


**GOATHERD**

No, shepherd,
            nothing doing;
                        it's not for us
to be heard during the noon hush.
            We dread Pan,
                        who for a fact
is stretched out somewhere,
            dog tired from the chase;
                        his mood is bitter,
anger ready at his nostrils.
            But, Thyrsis,
                        since you are good at

**103**

singing of *The Afflictions of Daphnis,*
        and have most deeply
               meditated the pastoral mode,
come here,
        let us sit down,
               under this elm
facing Priapus and the fountain fairies,
        here where the shepherds come
               to try themselves out
by the oak trees.
        Ah! may you sing
               as you sang that day
facing Chromis out of Libya,
        I will let you milk, yes,
               three times over,
a goat that is the mother of twins
        and even when
               she has sucked her kids
her milk fills
        two pails. I will give besides,
               new made, a two-eared bowl
of ivy-wood,
        rubbed with beeswax
               that smacks still
of the knife of the carver.
        Round its upper edges
               winds the ivy, ivy
flecked with yellow flowers
        and about it
               is twisted
a tendril joyful with the saffron fruit.
        Within,
               is limned a girl,
as fair a thing as the gods have made,
        dressed in a sweeping
               gown.

Her hair
                    is confined by a snood.
                                 Beside her
two fair-haired youths
                    with alternate speech
                                 are contending
but her heart is
                    untouched.
                                 Now,
she glances at one,
                    smiling,
                                 and now, lightly
she flings the other a thought,
                    while their eyes,
                                 by reason of love's
long vigils, are heavy
                    but their labors
                                 all in vain.
In addition
                    there is fashioned there
                                 an ancient fisherman
and a rock,
                    a rugged rock,
                                 on which
with might and main
                    the old man poises a great net
                                 for the cast
as one who puts his whole heart into it.
                    One would say
                                 that he was fishing
with the full strength of his limbs
                    so big do his muscles stand out
                                 about the neck.
Gray-haired though he be,
                    he has the strength
                                 of a young man.

Now, separated
            from the sea-broken old man
                        by a narrow interval
is a vineyard,
            heavy
                        with fire-red clusters,
and on a rude wall
            sits a small boy
                        guarding them.
Round him
            two she-foxes are skulking.
                        One
goes the length of the vine-rows
            to eat the grapes
                        while the other
brings all her cunning to bear,
            by what has been set down,
                        vowing
she will never quit the lad
            until
                        she leaves him bare
and breakfastless.
            But the boy
                        is plaiting a pretty
cage of locust stalks and asphodel,
            fitting in the reeds
                        and cares less for his scrip
and the vines
            than he takes delight
                        in his plaiting.
All about the cup
            is draped the mild acanthus
                        a miracle of varied work,
a thing for you to marvel at.
            I paid
                        a Caledonian ferryman

a goat and a great white
                    cream-cheese
                              for the bowl.
It is still virgin to me,
                    its lip has never touched mine.
                              To gain my desire,
I would gladly
                    give this cup
                              if you, my friend,
will sing for me
                    that delightful song.
                              I hold nothing back.
Begin, my friend,
                    for you cannot,
                              you may be sure,
take your song,
                    which drives all things out of mind,
                              with you to the other world.

## The Desert Music

—the dance begins: to end about a form
propped motionless—on the bridge
between Juárez and El Paso—unrecognizable
in the semi-dark

Wait!

The others waited while you inspected it,
on the very walk itself            .

Is it alive?

—neither a head,
legs nor arms!

It isn't a sack of rags someone
has abandoned here         .        torpid against
the flange of the supporting girder        .        ?

an inhuman shapelessness,
knees hugged tight up into the belly

Egg-shaped!

What a place to sleep!
on the International Boundary.    Where else,
interjurisdictional, not to be disturbed?

How shall we get said what must be said?

Only the poem.

Only the counted poem, to an exact measure:
to imitate, not to copy nature, not
to copy nature

NOT, prostrate, to copy nature
                              but a dance! to dance
two and two with him—
                    sequestered there asleep,
                              right end up!


     A music
supersedes his composure, hallooing to us
across a great distance   .   .

                         wakens the dance
who blows upon his benumbed fingers!

                         Only the poem
only the made poem, to get said what must
be said, not to copy nature, sticks
in our throats   .

The law?   The law gives us nothing
but a corpse, wrapped in a dirty mantle.
The law is based on murder and confinement,
long delayed,
but this, following the insensate music,
is based on the dance:

                    an agony of self-realization
bound into a whole
by that which surrounds us        .

                         I cannot escape

I cannot vomit it up

Only the poem!

Only the made poem, the verb calls it
                                    into being.


                        —it looks too small for a man.
A woman.   Or a very shriveled old man.
Maybe dead.   They probably inspect the place
and will cart it away later        .


                        Heave it into the river.
A good thing.

Leaving California to return east, the fertile desert,
                        (were it to get water)
surrounded us, a music of survival, subdued, distant, half
                        heard; we were engulfed
by it as in the early evening, seeing the wind lift
                        and drive the sand, we
passed Yuma. All night long, heading for El Paso to
                        meet our friend,
we slept fitfully.   Thinking of Paris, I waked to the tick
                        of the rails.   The
jagged desert        .


                                    —to tell
what subsequently I saw and what heard


                        —to place myself (in
my nature) beside nature


                        —to imitate
nature (for to copy nature would be a
        shameful thing)


                I lay myself down:

The Old Market's a good place to begin:
Let's cut through here—

                          tequila's only
a nickel a slug in these side streets.
Keep out though.   Oh, it's all right at
this time of day but I saw H. terribly
beaten up in one of those joints.   He
asked for it.   I thought he was going to
be killed.   I do
my drinking on the main drag   .

                    That's the bull ring
Oh, said Floss, after she got used to the
change of light   .
                 What color!   Isn't it
wonderful!

     —paper flowers (*para los santos*)
baked red-clay utensils, daubed
with blue, silverware,
dried peppers, onions, print goods, children's
clothing   .  the place deserted all but
for a few Indians squatted in the
booths, unnoticing (don't you think it)
as though they slept there    .

     There's a second tier.   Do you
want to go up?

     What makes Texans so tall?
We saw a woman this morning in a mink cape
six feet if she was an inch.   What a woman!

Probably a Broadway figure.

—tell you what else we saw: about a million
sparrows screaming their heads off

in the trees of that small park where
the buses stop, sanctuary,
I suppose,
from the wind driving the sand in that way
about the city     .

                    Texas rain they call it

—and those two alligators in the fountain     .

There were four

              I saw only two

                        They were looking
right at you all the time     .

Penny please!   Give me penny please, mister.

                    Don't give them anything.

                              .     instinctively
one has already drawn one's naked
wrist away from those obscene fingers
as in the mind a vague apprehension speaks
and the music rouses     .

                        Let's get in here.
              a music!    cut off as
the bar door closes behind us.

              We've got
another half hour.

              —returned to the street,
the pressure moves from booth to booth along

**112**

the curb.   Opposite, no less insistent
the better stores are wide open.   Come in
and look around.   You don't have to buy: hats,
riding boots, blankets     .

              Look at the way,
slung from her neck with a shawl, that young
Indian woman carries her baby!

              —a stream of Spanish,
as she brushes by, intense, wide-
eyed in eager talk with her boy husband

—three half-grown girls, one of them eating a
pomegranate.   Laughing.

                   and the serious tourist,
man and wife, middle-aged, middle-western,
their arms loaded with loot, whispering
together—still looking for bargains     .

                   and the aniline
red and green candy at the little booth
tended by the old Indian woman.
         Do you suppose anyone actually
buys—and eats the stuff?

My feet are beginning to ache me.

              We still got a few minutes.
Let's try here.   They had the mayor
up last month for taking $3000 a week from
the whorehouses of the city.   Not much left
for the girls.   There's a show on.

              Only a few tables
occupied.   A conventional orchestra—this

place livens up later—playing the usual local
jing-a-jing—a boy and girl team, she
                              confidential with someone
off stage.   Laughing: just finishing the act.

So we drink until the next turn—a strip tease.

Do you mean it?   Wow!   Look at her.

                              You'd have to be
pretty drunk to get any kick out of that.
She's no Mexican.   Some worn-out trouper from
the States.   Look at those breasts      .

          There is a fascination
          seeing her shake
          the beaded sequins from
          a string about her hips

          She gyrates but it's
          not what you think,
          one does not laugh
          to watch her belly.

          One is moved but not
          at the dull show.   The
          guitarist yawns.   She
          cannot even sing.    She

          has about her painted
          hardihood a screen
          of pretty doves which
          flutter their wings.

          Her cold eyes perfunc-
          torily moan but do not

smile.  Yet they bill
and coo by grace of
a certain candor.  She

is heavy on her feet.
That's good.  She
bends forward leaning
on the table of the
balding man sitting
upright, alone, so that
everything hangs for-
ward.
        What the hell
are you grinning
to yourself about?  Not
at *her?*
        The music!
I like her.  She fits

the music       .

Why don't these Indians get over this nauseating
prattle about their souls and their loves and sing
us something else for a change?

This place is rank
with it.  She
at least knows she's
part of another tune,
knows her customers,
has the same
opinion of them as I
have.  That gives her
one up    .      one up
following the lying
music       .

**115**

There is another music.   The bright-colored candy
of her nakedness lifts her unexpectedly
to partake of its tune         .


                              Andromeda of those rocks,
the virgin of her mind         .          those unearthly
greens and reds

                              in her mockery of virtue
she becomes unaccountably virtuous         .
                              though she in no
way pretends it         .


Let's get out of this.


                              In the street it hit
me in the face as we started to walk again.   Or
am I merely playing the poet?   Do I merely invent
it out of whole cloth?   I thought         .


             What in the form of an old whore in
             a cheap Mexican joint in Juárez, her bare
             can waggling crazily can be
             so refreshing to me, raise to my ear
             so sweet a tune, built of such slime?


             Here we are. They'll be along any minute.
             The bar is at the right of the entrance,
             a few tables opposite which you have to pass
             to get to the dining room, beyond.


             A foursome, two oversize Americans, no
             longer young, got up as cowboys,
             hats and all, are drunk and carrying on
             with their gals, drunk also,


             especially one inciting her man, the
             biggest, *Yip ee!* to dance in

the narrow space, oblivious to everything
—she is insatiable and he is trying

stumblingly to keep up with her.
Give it the gun, pardner! *Yip ee*!   We
pushed by them to our table, seven
of us.   Seated about the room

were quiet family groups, some with
children, eating.   Rather a better
class than you notice
on the streets.   So here we are.   You

can see through into the kitchen
where one of the cooks, his shirt sleeves
rolled up, an apron over
the well-pressed pants of a street

suit, black hair neatly parted,
a tall
good-looking man, is working
absorbed, before a chopping block

Old fashioneds all around?

                    So this is William
Carlos Williams, the poet          .

              Floss and I had half consumed
our quartered hearts of lettuce before
we noticed the others hadn't touched theirs          .
You seem quite normal.   Can you tell me?   Why
does one want to write a poem?

          Because it's there to be written.

**Oh.   A matter of inspiration then?**

                              Of necessity.

Oh.   But what sets it off?

            I am that he whose brains
            are scattered
                    aimlessly

                         —and so,
the hour done, the quail eaten, we were on
our way back to El Paso.

                      Good night.   Good
night and thank you  .  No. Thank you. We're
going to walk        .

—and so, on the naked wrist, we feel again
those insistent fingers        .

                      Penny please, mister.
Penny please.   Give me penny.

                      Here! now go away.

—but the music, the music has reawakened
as we leave the busier parts of the street
and come again to the bridge in the semi-dark,
pay our fee and begin again to cross      .
seeing the lights along the mountain back of El
Paso and pause to watch the boys calling out
to us to throw more coins to them standing
in the shallow water   .   so that's
where the incentive lay, with the annoyance
of those surprising fingers.

                      So you're a poet?
a good thing to be got rid of—half drunk,

a free dinner under your belt, even though you
get typhoid—and to have met people you
can at least talk to     .


        relief from that changeless, endless
inescapable and insistent music     .


        What else, Latins, do you yourselves
seek but relief!
with the expressionless ding dong you dish up
to us of your souls and your loves, which
we swallow. Spaniards! (though these are mostly
Indians who chase the white bastards
through the streets on their Independence Day
and try to kill them)     .


                What's that?


Oh, come on.


        But what's THAT?


            the music! the
*music*! as when Casals struck
and held a deep cello tone
and I am speechless     .


            There it sat
in the projecting angle of the bridge flange
as I stood aghast and looked at it—
in the half-light: shapeless or rather returned
to its original shape, armless, legless,
headless, packed like the pit of a fruit into
that obscure corner—or
a fish to swim against the stream—or
a child in the womb prepared to imitate life,

warding its life against
a birth of awful promise.   The music
guards it, a mucus, a film that surrounds it,
a benumbing ink that stains the
sea of our minds—to hold us off—shed
of a shape close as it can get to no shape,
a music! a protecting music         .

                              I *am* a poet! I
am.   I am.   I am a poet, I reaffirmed, ashamed

Now the music volleys through as in
a lonely moment I hear it.   Now it is all
about me.   The dance!   The verb detaches itself
seeking to become articulate         .

            And I could not help thinking
            of the wonders of the brain that
            hears that music and of our
            skill sometimes to record it.

# Journey to Love

*(1955)*

*For My Wife*

## A Negro Woman

carrying a bunch of marigolds
        wrapped
                in an old newspaper:
She carries them upright,
        bareheaded,
                the bulk
of her thighs
        causing her to waddle
                as she walks
looking into
        the store window which she passes
                on her way.
What is she
        but an ambassador
                from another world
a world of pretty marigolds
        of two shades
                which she announces
not knowing what she does
        other
                than walk the streets
holding the flowers upright
        as a torch
                so early in the morning.

## The Ivy Crown

The whole process is a lie,
    unless,
            crowned by excess,
it break forcefully,
    one way or another,
         from its confinement—
or find a deeper well.
    Antony and Cleopatra
        were right;
they have shown
    the way. I love you
        or I do not live
at all.

Daffodil time
    is past. This is
        summer, summer!
the heart says,
    and not even the full of it.
        No doubts
are permitted—
    though they will come
        and may
before our time
    overwhelm us.
        We are only mortal
but being mortal
    can defy our fate.
        We may
by an outside chance
    even win! We do not
        look to see
jonquils and violets

                come again
                            but there are,
        still,
                    the roses!


Romance has no part in it.
            The business of love is
                            cruelty *which*,
        by our wills,
                    we transform
                            to live together.
        It has its seasons,
                    for and against,
                            whatever the heart
        fumbles in the dark
                    to assert
                            toward the end of May.
        Just as the nature of briars
                    is to tear flesh,
                            I have proceeded
        through them.
                    Keep
                            the briars out,
        they say.
                    You cannot live
                            and keep free of
        briars.


Children pick flowers.
            Let them.
                            Though having them
        in hand
                    they have no further use for them
                            but leave them crumpled
        at the curb's edge.

At our age the imagination
                across the sorry facts
                            lifts us
to make roses
            stand before thorns.
                            Sure
love is cruel
            and selfish
                        and totally obtuse—
at least, blinded by the light,
            young love is.
                        But we are older,
I to love
            and you to be loved,
                    we have,
no matter how,
            by our wills survived
                        to keep
the jeweled prize
            always
                        at our finger tips.
We will it so
            and so it is
                        past all accident.

## View by Color Photography
## on a Commercial Calendar

The church of Vice-Morcate
        in the Canton Ticino
                with its apple blossoms
is beautiful
        as anything I have ever seen
                in or out of
Switzerland.
        The beauty of holiness
                the beauty of a man's anger
reflecting his sex
        or a woman's either,
                mountainous,
or a little stone church
        from a height
            or
close to the camera
        the apple tree in blossom
                or the far lake
below
        in the distance—
            are equal
as they are unsurpassed.
        Peace
            after the event
comes from their contemplation,
        a great peace.
            The sky is cut off,
there is no horizon
        just the mountainside
            bordered by water
on which tiny waves

                without passion
                            unconcerned
    cover the invisible fish.
                And who but we are concerned
                            with the beauty of apple blossoms
    and a small church
                on a promontory,
                            an ancient church—
    by the look of its masonry—
                abandoned
                            by a calm lake
    in the mountains
                where the sun shines
                            of a springtime
    afternoon. Something
                has come to an end here,
                            it has been accomplished.

# *The Sparrow*

*(To My Father)*


This sparrow
        who comes to sit at my window
                is a poetic truth
more than a natural one.
        His voice,
                his movements,
his habits—
        how he loves to
                flutter his wings
in the dust—
        all attest it;
                granted, he does it
to rid himself of lice
        but the relief he feels
                makes him
cry out lustily—
        which is a trait
                more related to music
than otherwise.
        Wherever he finds himself
                in early spring,
on back streets
        or beside palaces,
                he carries on
unaffectedly
        his amours.
                It begins in the egg,
his sex genders it:
        What is more pretentiously
                useless
or about which
        we more pride ourselves?

                    It leads as often as not
to our undoing.
                    The cockerel, the crow
                        with their challenging voices
cannot surpass
                    the insistence
                        of his cheep!
Once
            at El Paso
                    toward evening,
I saw—and heard!—
                    ten thousand sparrows
                        who had come in from
the desert
                    to roost. They filled the trees
                        of a small park. Men fled
(with ears ringing!)
                    from their droppings,
                        leaving the premises
to the alligators
                    who inhabit
                        the fountain. His image
is familiar
                    as that of the aristocratic
                        unicorn, a pity
there are not more oats eaten
                    nowadays
                        to make living easier
for him.
                    At that,
                        his small size,
keen eyes,
                    serviceable beak
                        and general truculence
assure his survival—
                    to say nothing
                        of his innumerable

brood.
            Even the Japanese
                know him
and have painted him
            sympathetically,
                with profound insight
into his minor
            characteristics.
                Nothing even remotely
subtle
            about his lovemaking.
                He crouches
before the female,
            drags his wings,
                waltzing,
throws back his head
            and simply—
                yells! The din
is terrific.
            The way he swipes his bill
                across a plank
to clean it,
            is decisive.
                So with everything
he does. His coppery
            eyebrows
                give him the air
of being always
            a winner—and yet
                I saw once,
the female of his species
            clinging determinedly
                to the edge of
a water pipe,
            catch him
                by his crown-feathers
to hold him

silent,
                    subdued,
hanging above the city streets
             until
                    she was through with him.
What was the use
             of that?
                    *She* hung there
herself,
             puzzled at her success.
                    I laughed heartily.
Practical to the end,
             it is the poem
                    of his existence
that triumphed
             finally;
                    a wisp of feathers
flattened to the pavement,
             wings spread symmetrically
                    as if in flight,
the head gone,
             the black escutcheon of the breast
                    undecipherable,
an effigy of a sparrow,
             a dried wafer only,
                    left to say
and it says it
             without offense,
                    beautifully;
This was I,
             a sparrow.
                    I did my best;
farewell.

## The King!

Nell Gwyn,
     it says in the dictionary,
          actress
and mistress of Charles the Second:
     what a lot
          of pious rot there is
surrounding
     that
          simple statement.
She waked in the morning,
     bathed in
          the King's bountiful
water
     which enveloped her
          completely and,
magically,
     with the grit, took away
          all her sins.
It was the King's body
     which was served;
          the King's boards which
in the evening
     she capably trod;
          she fed
the King's poor
     and when she died,
          left them some slight moneys
under certain
     conditions.

Happy the woman
     whose husband makes her
          the "King's whore."
All this you will find

in the dictionary
                    where it has been
preserved forever—
                    since it is beautiful
                        and true.


## The Lady Speaks


A storm raged among the live oaks
                    while my husband and I
                        sat in the semi-dark
listening!
                We watched from the windows,
                        the lights off,
saw the moss
            whipped upright
                    by the wind's force.
Two candles we had lit
                side by side
                        before us
so solidly had our house been built
                kept their tall flames
                        unmoved.
May it be so
                when a storm sends the moss
                        whipping
back and forth
            upright
                    above my head
like flames in the final
                fury.

## Tribute to the Painters

Satyrs dance!
          all the deformities take wing
                    centaurs
leading to the rout of the vocables
          in the writings
of Gertrude
          Stein—but
                    you cannot be
an artist
          by mere ineptitude     .
The dream
          is in pursuit!

The neat figures of
          Paul Klee
                    fill the canvas
but that
          is not the work
                    of a child     .
The cure began, perhaps,
          with the abstractions
                    of Arabic art
Dürer
          with his *Melancholy*
                    was ware of it—
the shattered masonry. Leonardo
          saw it,
                    the obsession,
and ridiculed it
          in *La Gioconda*.
                    Bosch's
congeries of tortured souls and devils
          who prey on them
                    fish

swallowing
            their own entrails
Freud
            Picasso
                        Juan Gris.
The letter from a friend
            saying:
                        For the last
three nights
            I have slept like a baby
                        without
liquor or dope of any sort!
            We know
                        that a stasis
from a chrysalis
            has stretched its wings—
                        like a bull
or the Minotaur
            or Beethoven
                        in the scherzo
of his 9th Symphony
            stomped
                        his heavy feet
I saw love
            mounted naked on a horse
                        on a swan
the back of a fish
            the bloodthirsty conger eel
                        and laughed
recalling the Jew
            in the pit
                        among his fellows
when the indifferent chap
            with the machine gun
                        was spraying the heap.

He
                had not yet been hit
                            but smiled
comforting his companions.

Dreams possess me
                and the dance
                            of my thoughts
involving animals
                the blameless beasts
and there came to me
                just now
                            the knowledge of
the tyranny of the image
                and how
                            men
in their designs
                have learned
                            to shatter it
whatever it may be,
                that the trouble
                            in their minds
shall be quieted,
                put to bed
                            again.

## To a Man Dying on His Feet

—not that we are not all
            "dying on our feet"
                        but the look you give me
and to which I bow,
                is more immediate.
                            It is keenly alert,
suspicious of me—
            as of all that are living—and
                        apologetic.
Your jaw
            wears the stubble
                        of a haggard beard,
a dirty beard,
            which resembles
                        the snow through which
your long legs
            are conducting you.
                        Whither? Where are you going?
This would be a fine day
            to go on a journey.
                        Say to Florida
where at this season
            all go
                        nowadays.
There grows the hibiscus,
            the star jasmine
                        and more than I can tell
but the odors
            from what I know
                        must be alluring.
Come with me there!
            you look like a good guy,
                        come this evening.

The plane leaves at 6:30
                or have you another
                                appointment?


## Come on!


A different kind of thought
                blander
                                and more desperate
like that of
                Sergeant So-and-So
                                at the road
in Belleau Wood:
                Come on!
                                Do you want to live
forever?—
                That
                                is the essence
of poetry.
                But it does not
                                always
take the same form.
                For the most part
                                it consists
in listening
                to the nightingale
                                or fools.

**139**

## The Pink Locust

I'm persistent as the pink locust,
            once admitted
                        to the garden,
you will not easily get rid of it.
                  Tear it from the ground,
                              if one hair-thin rootlet
remain
            it will come again.
                        It is
flattering to think of myself
                  so. It is also
                              laughable.
A modest flower,
                  resembling a pink sweet-pea,
                              you cannot help
but admire it
                  until its habits
                              become known.
Are we not most of us
                  like that? It would be
                              too much
if the public
                  pried among the minutiae
                              of our private affairs.
Not
                  that we have anything to hide
                              but could *they*
stand it? Of course
                  the world would be gratified
                              to find out
what fools we have made of ourselves.
                  The question is,
                              would they

be generous with us—
        as we have been
                with others? It is,
as I say,
      a flower
           incredibly resilient
under attack!
        Neglect it
           and it will grow into a tree.
I wish I could *so* think of myself
        and of what
           is to become of me.
The poet himself,
        what does he think of himself
           facing his world?
It will not do to say,
        as he is inclined to say:
           Not much. The poem
would be in *that* betrayed.
        He might as well answer—
        "a rose is a rose
is a rose" and let it go at that.
        A rose *is* a rose
           and the poem equals it
if it be well made.
        The poet
        cannot slight himself
without slighting
        his poem—
           which would be
ridiculous.
        Life offers
           no greater reward.
And so,
        like this flower,
           I persist—

for what there may be in it.
                I am not,
                            I know,
in the galaxy of poets
                a rose
                            but *who*, among the rest,
will deny me
                my place.


## Classic Picture


It is a classic picture,
                women have always fussed with their hair
                            (having no sisters
I never watched the process
                so intimately
                            as this time); the reason for it
is not clear—
                tho' I acknowledge,
                            an unkempt head of hair,
while not as repulsive as a nest of snakes,
                is repulsive enough
                            in a woman.
Therefore
                she fusses with her hair
                            for
a woman does not want to seem repulsive,
                unless      .
                            to gain for herself      .

she be hungry,
            hungry!
                    as would be a man
and all hunger is repulsive
            and puts on
                    an ugly face.
Their heads are not made as a man's,
            an ornament
                    in itself. They have
other charms—
            needless
                    to enumerate. Under
their ornate coiffures
            lurks a specter,
                    coiling snakes
doubling for tresses        .

A woman's brains
            which can be keen
                    are condemned,
like a poet's,
            to what deceptions she can muster
                    to lead men
to their ruin.
            But look more deeply
                    into her maneuvers,
and puzzle as we will about them
            they may mean
                    anything        .

## Address:

To a look in my son's eyes—
        I hope he did not see
                that I was looking—
that I have seen
        often enough
                in the mirror,
a male look
        approaching despair—
                there is a female look
to match it
        no need to speak of that:
                Perhaps
it was only a dreamy look
        not an unhappy one
                but absent
from the world—
        such as plagued the eyes
                of Bobby Burns
in his youth and threw him
        into the arms
                of women—
in which he could
        forget himself,
                not defiantly,
but with full acceptance
        of his lot
                as a man   .   .
His Jean forgave him
        and took him to her heart
                time after time
when he would be
        too drunk
                with Scotch

**144**

or the love of other women
        to notice
                what he was doing.
What was he intent upon
        but to drown out
                that look? What
does it portend?
        A war
                will not erase it
nor a bank account,
        estlin,
                amounting to 9 figures.
Flow gently sweet Afton
        among thy green braes—
                no matter
that he wrote the song
        to another woman
                it was never for sale.

## The Drunk and the Sailor

The petty fury
　　　　that disrupts my life—
　　　　　　　at the striking of a wrong key
as if it had been
　　　　a woman lost
or a fortune　　.　　.
　　　　　　The man was obviously drunk,
　　　　　　　　Christopher Marlowe
could have been no drunker
　　　　when he got himself
　　　　　　　stuck through the eye
with a poniard.
　　　　　　The bus station was crowded.
The man
　　　　heavy-set
　　　　　　about my own age
seventy
　　　　was talking privately
　　　　　　with a sailor.
He had an ugly jaw on him.
　　　　　　Suddenly
　　　　　　　sitting there on the bench
too drunk to stand
　　　　he began menacingly
　　　　　　his screaming.
The young sailor
　　　　who could have flattened him
　　　　　　at one blow
kept merely looking at him.
　　　　　　The nerve-tingling screeches
　　　　　　　that sprang
*sforzando*
　　　　from that stubble beard

                    would have distinguished
an operatic tenor.
            But me—
                    the shock of it—
my heart leaped in my chest
            so that I saw red
                    wanted
to strangle the guy     .
            The fury of love
                    is no less.

## A Smiling Dane

The Danish native
            before the Christian era
                        whose body
features intact
            with a rope
                        also intact
round the neck
            found recently
                        in a peat bog
is dead.
                        Are you surprised?
                        You should be.
The diggers
            who discovered him
                        expected more.
Frightened
            they quit the place
                        thinking
his ghost might walk.

The cast of his features
            shows him
                        to be
a man of intelligence.
            It did him no good.
                        What his eyes saw
cannot be more
            than the male
                        and female
of it—
            if as much.
                        His stomach
its contents examined
            shows him
                        before he died

to have had
                a meal
                                consisting of local grains
swallowed whole
                which he probably enjoyed
                                though he did not
much as we do
                chew them.
                                And what if
the image of his frightened executioners
                is not recorded?
                                Do we not know
their features
                as if
                                it had occurred
today?
                We can still see in his smile
                                their grimaces.

## Shadows

Shadows cast by the street light
          under the stars,
                    the head is tilted back,
the long shadow of the legs
          presumes a world
                    taken for granted
on which the cricket trills.
          The hollows of the eyes
                    are unpeopled.
Right and left
          climb the ladders of night
                    as dawn races
to put out the stars.
          That
                    is the poetic figure
but we know
          better: what is not now
                    will never
be. Sleep secure,
          the little dog in the snapshot
                    keeps his shrewd eyes
pared. Memory
          is liver than sight.
                    A man
looking out,
          seeing the shadows—
                    it is himself
that can be painlessly amputated
          by a mere shifting
                    of the stars.
A comfort so easily not to be

and to be at once one
                    with every man.
The night blossoms
          with a thousand shadows
                              so long
as there are stars,
                street lights
                              or a moon and
who shall say
              by their shadows
which is different
                from the other
                              fat or lean.


                    II


Ripped from the concept of our lives
                and from all concept
                              somehow, and plainly,
the sun will come up
                each morning
                              and sink again.
So that we experience
                violently
                              every day
two worlds
              one of which we share with the
              rose in bloom
                              and one,
by far the greater,
                with the past,
                              the world of memory,
the silly world of history,
                the world
                              of the imagination.

Which leaves only the beasts and trees,
          crystals
                    with their refractive
                    surfaces
and rotting things
          to stir our wonder.
                    Save for the little
central hole
          of the eye itself
                    into which
we dare not stare too hard
          or we are lost.
                    The instant
trivial as it is
          is all we have
                    unless—unless
things the imagination feeds upon,
          the scent of the rose,
                    startle us anew.

# Asphodel, That Greeny Flower

BOOK I

Of asphodel, that greeny flower,
>> like a buttercup
>>> upon its branching stem—
save that it's green and wooden—
>> I come, my sweet,
>>> to sing to you.
We lived long together
>> a life filled,
>>> if you will,
with flowers. So that
>> I was cheered
>>> when I came first to know
that there were flowers also
>> in hell.
>>> Today
I'm filled with the fading memory of those flowers
>> that we both loved,
>>> even to this poor
colorless thing—
>> I saw it
>>> when I was a child—
little prized among the living
>> but the dead see,
>>> asking among themselves:
What do I remember
>> that was shaped
>>> as this thing is shaped?
while our eyes fill
>> with tears.
>>> Of love, abiding love
it will be telling

**153**

                    though too weak a wash of crimson
                              colors it
        to make it wholly credible.
                    There is something
                              something urgent
    I have to say to you
                    and you alone
                              but it must wait
        while I drink in
                    the joy of your approach,
                              perhaps for the last time.
    And so
                    with fear in my heart
                              I drag it out
        and keep on talking
                    for I dare not stop.
                              Listen while I talk on
        against time.
                    It will not be
                              for long.
    I have forgot      .
                    and yet I see clearly enough
                              something
        central to the sky
                    which ranges round it.
                              An odor
        springs from it!
                    A sweetest odor!
                              Honeysuckle! And now
        there comes the buzzing of a bee!
                    and a whole flood
                              of sister memories!
        Only give me time,
                    time to recall them
                              before I shall speak out.
        Give me time,
                    time.

When I was a boy
            I kept a book
                        to which, from time
to time,
            I added pressed flowers
                        until, after a time,
I had a good collection.
            The asphodel,
                        forebodingly,
among them.
            I bring you,
                        reawakened,
a memory of those flowers.
            They were sweet
                        when I pressed them
and retained
            something of their sweetness
                        a long time.
It is a curious odor,
            a moral odor,
                        that brings me
near to you.
            The color
                        was the first to go.
There had come to me
            a challenge,
                        your dear self,
mortal as I was,
            the lily's thoat
                        to the hummingbird!
Endless wealth,
            I thought,
                        held out its arms to me.
A thousand topics
            in an apple blossom.
                        The generous earth itself

gave us lief.
                The whole world
                        became my garden!
But the sea
            which no one tends
                    is also a garden
when the sun strikes it
            and the waves
                    are wakened.
I have seen it
            and so have you
                    when it puts all flowers
to shame.
                Too, there are the starfish
                    stiffened by the sun
and other sea wrack
            and weeds. We knew that
                    along with the rest of it
for we were born by the sea,
            knew its rose hedges
                    to the very water's brink.
There the pink mallow grows
            and in their season
                    strawberries
and there, later,
            we went to gather
                    the wild plum.
I cannot say
            that I have gone to hell
                    for your love
but often
            found myself there
                    in your pursuit.
I do not like it
            and wanted to be
                    in heaven. Hear me out.

Do not turn away.

I have learned much in my life
    from books
        and out of them
about love.
    Death
        is not the end of it.
There is a hierarchy
    which can be attained,
        I think,
in its service.
    Its guerdon
        is a fairy flower;
a cat of twenty lives.
    If no one came to try it
        the world
would be the loser.
    It has been
        for you and me
as one who watches a storm
    come in over the water.
        We have stood
from year to year
    before the spectacle of our lives
        with joined hands.
The storm unfolds.
    Lightning
        plays about the edges of the clouds.
The sky to the north
    is placid,
        blue in the afterglow
as the storm piles up.
    It is a flower
        that will soon reach
the apex of its bloom.
    We danced,

in our minds,
and read a book together.
                    You remember?
                              It was a serious book.
And so books
              entered our lives.
The sea! The sea!
              Always
                        when I think of the sea
there comes to mind
              the *Iliad*
                        and Helen's public fault
that bred it.
              Were it not for that
                        there would have been
no poem but the world
              if we had remembered,
                        those crimson petals
spilled among the stones,
              would have called it simply
                        murder.
The sexual orchid that bloomed then
              sending so many
                        disinterested
men to their graves
              has left its memory
                        to a race of fools
or heroes
              if silence is a virtue.
                        The sea alone
with its multiplicity
              holds any hope.
                        The storm
has proven abortive
              but we remain
                        after the thoughts it roused

to
              re-cement our lives.
                     It is the mind
the mind
            that must be cured
                    short of death's
intervention,
            and the will becomes again
                    a garden. The poem
is complex and the place made
            in our lives
                    for the poem.
Silence can be complex too,
            but you do not get far
                    with silence.
Begin again.
            It is like Homer's
                    catalogue of ships:
it fills up the time.
            I speak in figures,
                    well enough, the dresses
you wear are figures also,
            we could not meet
                    otherwise. When I speak
of flowers
            it is to recall
                    that at one time
we were young.
            All women are not Helen,
                    I know that,
but have Helen in their hearts.
            My sweet,
                    you have it also, therefore
I love you
            and could not love you otherwise.
                    Imagine you saw

a field made up of women
		all silver-white.
					What should you do
but love them?
			The storm bursts
				or fades! it is not
the end of the world.
			Love is something else,
				or so I thought it,
a garden which expands,
			though I knew you as a woman
				and never thought otherwise,
until the whole sea
			has been taken up
				and all its gardens.
It was the love of love,
			the love that swallows up all else,
				a grateful love,
a love of nature, of people,
			animals,
				a love engendering
gentleness and goodness
			that moved me
				and *that* I saw in you.
I should have known
			though I did not,
				that the lily-of-the-valley
is a flower makes many ill
			who whiff it.
				We had our children,
rivals in the general onslaught.
			I put them aside
				though I cared for them
as well as any man
			could care for his children
				according to my lights.

You understand
          I had to meet you
                    after the event
and have still to meet you.
          Love
                    to which you too shall bow
along with me—
          a flower
                    a weakest flower
shall be our trust
          and not because
                    we are too feeble
to do otherwise
          but because
                    at the height of my power
I risked what I had to do,
          therefore to prove
                    that we love each other
while my very bones sweated
          that I could not cry to you
                    in the act.
Of asphodel, that greeny flower,
          I come, my sweet,
                    to sing to you!
My heart rouses
          thinking to bring you news
                    of something
that concerns you
          and concerns many men. Look at
                    what passes for the new.
You will not find it there but in
          despised poems.
                    It is difficult
to get the news from poems
          yet men die miserably every day
                    for lack

**161**

of what is found there.
            Hear me out
                        for I too am concerned
and every man
            who wants to die at peace in his bed
                        besides.




BOOK II

Approaching death,
            as we think, the death of love,
                        no distinction
any more suffices to differentiate
            the particulars
                        of place and condition
with which we have been long
            familiar.
                        All appears
as if seen
            wavering through water.
                        We start awake with a cry
of recognition
            but soon the outlines
                        become again vague.
If we are to understand our time,
            we must find the key to it,
                        not in the eighteenth
and nineteenth centuries,
            but in earlier, wilder
                        and darker epochs    .    .
So to know, what I have to know
            about my own death,
                        if it be real,

I have to take it apart.
                    What does your generation think
                            of Cézanne?
I asked a young artist.
                    The abstractions of Hindu painting,
                            he replied,
is all at the moment which interests me.
                    He liked my poem
                            about the parts
of a broken bottle,
                    lying green in the cinders
                            of a hospital courtyard.
There was also, to his mind,
                    the one on gay wallpaper
                            which he had heard about
but not read.
                    I was grateful to him
                            for his interest.

Do you remember
                    how at Interlaken
                            we were waiting, four days,
to see the Jungfrau
                    but rain had fallen steadily.
                            Then
just before train time
                    on a tip from one of the waitresses
                            we rushed
to the Gipfel Platz
                    and there it was!
                            in the distance
covered with new-fallen snow.
                    When I was at Granada,
                            I remember,
in the overpowering heat
                    climbing a treeless hill
                            overlooking the Alhambra.

At my appearance at the summit
　　　　　two small boys
　　　　　　　　who had been playing
there
　　　　　made themselves scarce.
　　　　　　　　　　　Starting to come down
by a new path
　　　　　I at once found myself surrounded
　　　　　　　　　by gypsy women
who came up to me,
　　　　　I could speak little Spanish,
　　　　　　　　and directed me,
guided by a young girl,
　　　　on my way.
　　　　　　　　　These were the pinnacles.
The deaths I suffered
　　　　　began in the heads
　　　　　　　　about me, my eyes
were too keen
　　　　not to see through
　　　　　　　the world's niggardliness.
I accepted it
　　　　as my fate.
　　　　　　　　The wealthy
I defied
　　　　or not so much they,
　　　　　　　　for they have their uses,
as they who take their cues from them.
　　　　　I lived
　　　　　　　to breathe above the stench
not knowing how I in my own person
　　　　　would be overcome
　　　　　　　　finally. I was lost
failing the poem.
　　　　　But if I have come from the sea
　　　　　　　it is not to be

wholly
        fascinated by the glint of waves.
             The free interchange
of light over their surface
        which I have compared
             to a garden
should not deceive us
        or prove
             too difficult a figure.
The poem
        if it reflects the sea
             reflects only
its dance
        upon that profound depth
             where
it seems to triumph.
        The bomb puts an end
             to all that.
I am reminded
        that the bomb
             also
is a flower
        dedicated
             howbeit
to our destruction.
        The mere picture
             of the exploding bomb
fascinates us
        so that we cannot wait
             to prostrate ourselves
before it. We do not believe
        that love
             can so wreck our lives.
The end
        will come
             in its time.

Meanwhile
        we are sick to death
                of the bomb
and its childlike
        insistence.
                Death is no answer,
no answer—
        to a blind old man
                whose bones
have the movement
        of the sea,
                a sexless old man
for whom it is a sea
        of which his verses
                are made up.
There is no power
        so great as love
                which is a sea,
which is a garden—
        as enduring
                as the verses
of that blind old man
        destined
                to live forever.
Few men believe that
        nor in the games of children.
                They believe rather
in the bomb
        and shall die by
                the bomb.
Compare Darwin's voyage of the *Beagle*,
        a voyage of discovery if there ever was one,
                to the death
incommunicado
        in the electric chair
                of the Rosenbergs.

It is the mark of the times
                    that though we condemn
                                        what they stood for
we admire their fortitude.
                    But Darwin
                                        opened our eyes
to the gardens of the world,
                    as *they* closed them.
                                        Or take that other voyage
which promised so much
                    but due to the world's avarice
                                        breeding  hatred
through fear,
                    ended so disastrously;
                                        a voyage
with which I myself am so deeply concerned,
                    that of the *Pinta,*
                                        the *Niña*
and the *Santa María.*
                    How the world opened its eyes!
                                        It was a flower
upon which April
                    had descended from the skies!
                                        How bitter
a disappointment!
                    In all,
                                        this led mainly
to the deaths I have suffered.
                    For there had been kindled
                                        more minds
than that of the discoverers
                    and set dancing
                                        to a measure,
a new measure!
                    Soon lost.
                                        The measure itself

has been lost
                    and we suffer for it.
                              We come to our deaths
in silence.
                    The bomb speaks.
                              All suppressions,
from the witchcraft trials at Salem
                    to the latest
                              book burnings
are confessions
                    that the bomb
                              has entered our lives
to destroy us.
                    Every drill
                              driven into the earth
for oil enters my side
                    also.
                              Waste, waste!
dominates the world.
                    It is the bomb's work.
                              What else was the fire
at the Jockey Club in Buenos Aires
                    (*malos aires,* we should say)
                              when with Perón's connivance
the hoodlums destroyed,
                    along with the books
                              the priceless Goyas
that hung there?
                    You know how we treasured
                              the few paintings
we still cling to
                    especially the one
                              by the dead
Charlie Demuth.
                    With your smiles
                              and other trivia of the sort

my secret life
        has been made up,
                some baby's life
which had been lost
        had I not intervened.
                But the words
made solely of air
        or less,
                that came to me
out of the air
        and insisted
                on being written down,
I regret most—
        that there has come an end
                to them.
For in spite of it all,
        all that I have brought on myself,
                grew that single image
that I adore
        equally with you
                and so
it brought us together.


BOOK III

What power has love but forgiveness?
        In other words
                by its intervention
what has been done
        can be undone.
                What good is it otherwise?
Because of this
        I have invoked the flower
                in that

frail as it is
        after winter's harshness
            it comes again
to delect us.
        Asphodel, the ancients believed,
           in hell's despite
was such a flower.
        With daisies pied
           and violets blue,
we say, the spring of the year
        comes in!
           So may it be
with the spring of love's year
        also
           if we can but find
the secret word
        to transform it.
           It is ridiculous
what airs we put on
        to seem profound
           while our hearts
gasp dying
        for want of love.
           Having your love
I was rich.
        Thinking to have lost it
           I am tortured
and cannot rest.
        I do not come to you
           abjectly
with confessions of my faults,
        I have confessed,
           all of them.
In the name of love
        I come proudly
           as to an equal

to be forgiven.
                Let me, for I know
                        you take it hard,
with good reason,
                give the steps
                        if it may be
by which you shall mount,
                again to think well
                        of me.
The statue
                of Colleoni's horse
                        with the thickset little man
on top
                in armor
                        presenting a naked sword
comes persistently
                to my mind.
                        And with him
the horse rampant
                roused by the mare in
                        the Venus and Adonis.
These are pictures
                of crude force.
                        Once at night
waiting at a station
                with a friend
                        a fast freight
thundered through
                kicking up the dust.
                        My friend,
a distinguished artist,
                turned with me
                        to protect his eyes:
That's what we'd all like to be, Bill,
                he said. I smiled
                        knowing how deeply

he meant it. I saw another man
                yesterday
                        in the subway.
I was on my way uptown
           to a meeting.
                        He kept looking at me
and I at him:
                He had a worn knobbed stick
                      between his knees
suitable
           to keep off dogs,
                      a man of perhaps forty.
He wore a beard
           parted in the middle,
                a black beard,
and a hat,
           a brown felt hat
                lighter than
his skin. His eyes,
           which were intelligent,
                were wide open
but evasive, mild.
                I was frankly curious
                    and looked at him
closely. He was slight of build
           but robust enough
                had on
a double-breasted black coat
           and a vest
                which showed at the neck
the edge of a heavy and very dirty
           undershirt.
                His trousers
were striped
           and a lively
                reddish brown. His shoes

which were good
           if somewhat worn
                      had been recently polished.
His brown socks
           were about his ankles.
                      In his breast pocket
he carried
           a gold fountain pen
                      and a mechanical
pencil. For some reason
           which I could not fathom
                      I was unable
to keep my eyes off him.
           A worn leather zipper case
                      bulging with its contents
lay between his ankles
           on the floor.
                      Then I remembered:
When my father was a young man—
           it came to me
                      from an old photograph—
he wore such a beard.
           This man
                      reminds me of my father.
I am looking
           into my father's
                      face! Some surface
of some advertising sign
           is acting
                      as a reflector. It is
my own.
           But at once
                      the car grinds to a halt.
Speak to him,
           I cried. He
                      will know the secret.

He was gone
        and I did nothing about it.
               With him
went all men
        and all women too
               were in his loins.
Fanciful or not
        it seemed to me
               a flower
whose savor had been lost.
        It was a flower
               some exotic orchid
that Herman Melville had admired
        in the
               Hawaiian jungle.
Or the lilacs
        of men who left their marks,
               by torchlight,
rituals of the hunt,
        on the walls
               of prehistoric
caves in the Pyrenees—
        what draftsmen they were—
               bison and deer.
Their women
        had big buttocks.
               But what
draftsmen they were!
        By my father's beard,
               what draftsmen.
And so, by chance,
        how should it be otherwise?
               from what came to me
in a subway train
        I build a picture
               of all men.

It is winter
        and there
                waiting for you to care for them
are your plants.
        Poor things! you say
           as you compassionately
pour at their roots
      the reviving water.
           Lean-cheeked
I say to myself
      kindness moves her
          shall she not be kind
also to me? At this
      courage possessed me finally
         to go on.
Sweet, creep into my arms!
     I spoke hurriedly
         in the spell
of some wry impulse
      when I boasted
        that there was
any pride left in me.
     Do not believe it.
        Unless
in a special way,
     a way I shrink to speak of
        I am proud. After that manner
I call on you
     as I do on myself the same
       to forgive all women
who have offended you.
     It is the artist's failing
       to seek and to yield
such forgiveness.
     It will cure us both.
       Let us

keep it to ourselves but trust it.
         These heads
               that stick up all around me
are, I take it,
         also proud.
               But the flowers
know at least this much,
         that it is not spring
             and will be proud only
in the proper season.
         A trance holds men.
             They are dazed
and their faces in the public print
         show it. We follow them
             as children followed
the Pied Piper
         of Hamelin—but he
             was primarily
interested only in rats.
         I say to you
             privately
that the heads of most men I see
         at meetings
             or when I come up against them
elsewhere
         are full of cupidity.
             Let us breed
from those others.
         They are the flowers of the race.
             The asphodel
poor as it is
         is among them.
             But in their pride
there come to my mind
         the daisy,
             not the shy flower

of England but the brilliance
        that mantled
                with white
the fields
        which we knew
                as children.
Do you remember
        their spicy-sweet
                odor? What abundance!
There are many other flowers
        I could recall
                for your pleasure:
the small yellow sweet-scented violet
        that grew
                in marshy places!
You were like those
        though I quickly
                correct myself
for you were a woman
        and no flower
                and had to face
the problems which confront a woman.
        But you were for all that
                flowerlike
and I say this to you now
        and it is the thing
                which compounded
my torment
        that I never
                forgot it.
You have forgiven me
        making me new again.
                So that here
in the place
        dedicated in the imagination
                to memory

of the dead
            I bring you
                        a last flower. Don't think
that because I say this
            in a poem
                        it can be treated lightly
or that the facts will not uphold it.
            Are facts not flowers
                        and flowers facts
or poems flowers
            or all works of the imagination,
                        interchangeable?
Which proves
            that love
                        rules them all, for then
you will be my queen,
            my queen of love
                        forever more.


CODA

Inseparable from the fire
            its light
                        takes precedence over it.
Then follows
            what we have dreaded—
                        but it can never
overcome what has gone before.
            In the huge gap
                        between the flash
and the thunderstroke
            spring has come in
                        or a deep snow fallen.
Call it old age.
            In that stretch
                        we have lived to see

a colt kick up his heels.
                Do not hasten
                        laugh and play
in an eternity
                the heat will not overtake the light.
                        That's sure.
That gelds the bomb,
                permitting
                        that the mind contain it.
This is that interval,
                that sweetest interval,
                        when love will blossom,
come early, come late
                and give itself to the lover.
Only the imagination is real!
                I have declared it
                        time without end.
If a man die
                it is because death
                        has first
possessed his imagination.
                But if he refuse death—
                        no greater evil
can befall him
                unless it be the death of love
                        meet him
in full career.
                Then indeed
                        for him
the light has gone out.
But love and the imagination
                are of a piece,
                        swift as the light
to avoid destruction.
                So we come to watch time's flight
                        as we might watch

summer lightning
            or fireflies, secure,
                        by grace of the imagination,
safe in its care.
            For if
                        the light itself
has escaped,
            the whole edifice opposed to it
                        goes down.
Light, the imagination
            and love,
                        in our age,
by natural law,
            which we worship,
                        maintain
all of a piece
            their dominance.
So let us love
            confident as is the light
                        in its struggle with darkness
that there is as much to say
            and more
                        for the one side
and that not the darker
            which John Donne
                        for instance
among many men
            presents to us.
                        In the controversy
touching the younger
            and the older Tolstoi,
                        Villon, St. Anthony, Kung,
Rimbaud, Buddha
            and Abraham Lincoln
                        the palm goes
always to the light;

Who most shall advance the light—
call it what you may!
The light
for all time shall outspeed
the thunder crack.
Medieval pageantry
is human and we enjoy
the rumor of it
as in our world we enjoy
the reading of Chaucer,
likewise
a priest's raiment
(or that of a savage chieftain).
It is all
a celebration of the light.
All the pomp and ceremony
of weddings,
"Sweet Thames, run softly
till I end
my song,"—
are of an equal sort.
For our wedding, too,
the light was wakened
and shone. The light!
the light stood before us
waiting!
I thought the world
stood still.
At the altar
so intent was I
before my vows,
so moved by your presence
a girl so pale
and ready to faint
that I pitied
and wanted to protect you.

As I think of it now,
        after a lifetime,
                it is as if
a sweet-scented flower
        were poised
                and for me did open.
Asphodel
        has no odor
                save to the imagination
but it too
        celebrates the light.
                It is late
but an odor
        as from our wedding
                has revived for me
and begun again to penetrate
        into all crevices
                of my world.

## Ten Years of a New Rhythm

These poems were written over a period of less than ten years: the earliest, perhaps, is "To the Ghost of Marjorie Kinnan Rawlings," who died in 1953; "Heel and Toe" was written in 1961. Most of them utilize the triadic stanza and the "measured line," a discovery Dr. Williams made in *Paterson II*, beginning with "The descent beckons / as the ascent beckons," exhibited here in regular form in *Pictures from Brueghel*. I say "regular form," but, of course, Dr. Williams has adhered to no regular form since his *Poems: 1909*. With the Imagists, he practiced free verse; but in 1924 he rejected free verse ("This Florida") and sought for a controlled measure. This measure he was not to find until *Paterson*, developing the "variable foot" which produced *versos sueltos*, "loose verses," as he called them.

There was the danger that even with the "variable foot," the triadic stanza might become monotonous as free verse had become monotonous. It was "measure" that rescued Williams' verse by rhythmical variations, as the blank verse of Shakespeare and Milton was rescued by rhythmical variations of iambic pentameter. "The iamb is not the normal measure of American speech," he told me in 1953. "The foot has to be expanded or contracted in terms of actual speech. The key to modern poetry is *measure*, which must reflect the flux of modern life. You should find a variable measure for the fixed measure; for man and the poet must keep pace with this world."

Adhering quite rigorously to the triad in *Desert Music* and *Journey to Love*, Williams found that this form, even when measured, could not completely express the modern idiom. "The Gossips," one of the latest of these poems, runs to the sonnet length of fourteen lines (in form, of course, it is anything but a sonnet); "The Stone Crock" and "Poem—On Getting a Card ... from a Poet I Love" (E. E. Cummings) use the triadic pattern with a short fourth line to fill out the measure; "The Dance" and "Portrait of a Woman at Her Bath" run in almost regular quatrain form; "Some Simple Measures in the American Idiom and the Variable Foot" vary from verse form to verse form, controlled always, however, by the measure of the "variable foot." "Tapiola" (1959), looks and sounds suspiciously like free verse.

"How shall we get said what must be said?" Williams asks in *The Desert Music*: "Only the poem. / Only the counted poem, to an exact measure:" is his answer.

As he refined his measured line, Williams' poetry continued to improve. Many critics find some of his best poems written in the last ten years. Indeed, this crowning measure of his poetic line led Kenneth Rexroth to call him "the first American classic": ". . . his poetic line is organically welded to American speech like muscle to bone, as the choruses of Euripides were welded to the speech of the Athenians in the market place."

JOHN C. THIRLWALL
*The City College of New York*

# NEW DIRECTIONS PAPERBOOKS

Henry Miller, *The Colossus of Maroussi*. P 75
Henry Miller, *The Cosmological Eye*. P 109
Henry Miller, *Remember to Remember*. P 111
Henry Miller, *Sunday After the War*. P 110
Henry Miller, *The Time of the Assassins*. P 115
Henry Miller, *The Wisdom of the Heart*. P 94
Vladimir Nabokov, *Nikolai Gogol*. P 78
*New Directions, 11*, Anthology. P 72
*New Directions 16*, Anthology. P 64
*New Directions 17*, Anthology. P 103
Boris Pasternak, *Safe Conduct*. P 77
Kenneth Patchen, *Because It Is*. P 83
Kenneth Patchen, *The Journal of Albion Moonlight*. P 99
Ezra Pound, *ABC of Reading*. P 89
Ernest Fenollosa & Ezra Pound, *The Classic Noh Theatre of Japan*.
    P 79
Ezra Pound, *The Confucian Odes*. P 81
Ezra Pound, *Selected Poems*. P 66
Philip Rahv, *Image and Idea*. P 67
Kenneth Rexroth, *Assays*. P 113
Kenneth Rexroth, *Bird in the Bush*. P 80
Arthur Rimbaud, *Illuminations*. P 56
Arthur Rimbaud, *A Season in Hell & The Drunken Boat*. P 97
Jean-Paul Sartre, *Nausea*. P 82
Stendhal, *Lucien Leuwen, Book I: The Green Huntsman*. P 107
Stendhal, *Lucien Leuwen, Book II: The Telegraph*. P 108
Dylan Thomas, *A Child's Christmas in Wales*. Gift Edition,
    Out of Series
Dylan Thomas, *Portrait of the Artist as a Young Dog*. P 51
Dylan Thomas, *Quite Early One Morning*. P 90
Dylan Thomas, *Under Milk Wood*. P 73
William Carlos Williams, *In the American Grain*. P 53
William Carlos Williams, *The Farmers' Daughters*. P 106
William Carlos Williams, *Pictures from Brueghel and Other
    Poems*. P 118

Send for free catalogue describing all Paperbooks
NEW DIRECTIONS 333 Sixth Avenue New York 14